Reallocation

Strategies for Effective Resource Management

James A. Hyatt

Carol Herrnstadt Shulman

Aurora A. Santiago

NACUBO

Library of Congress Cataloging in Publication Data
Hyatt, James A., 1949–
    Reallocation: strategies for effective resource management.

    1. Public universities and colleges—Washington (State)—Finance—Case
studies. 2. Public universities and colleges—Michigan—Finance—Case
studies. 3. State aid to higher education—Washington (State). 4. State aid
to higher education—Michigan. 5. Public universities and colleges—Idaho—
Finance—Case studies. 6. State aid to higher education—Idaho.
I. Shulman, Carol Herrnstadt. II. Santiago, Aurora A. III. Title.
LB2328.6.H93 1984   379.1′214′0973   84-14888
ISBN 0-915164-21-3

Edited by Lanora Welzenbach

Contents

Foreword

Colleges and universities currently face the challenge of providing quality programs in a time of fiscal constraints. In an effort to provide guidance in meeting this challenge, NACUBO conducted a study of five public institutions that responded to fiscal stress. While the study initially focused on retrenchment, its results demonstrate the importance of reallocation as a long-term response to insure an institution's academic vitality. Thus, the results of this study have important implications for both public and independent institutions.

Thorough review of the experiences of the institutions encompassed by this study can provide valuable guidance to colleges and universities in responding to retrenchment and in the development of a responsive reallocation process. It is our firm belief that reallocation is an integral component of college and university financial management. A dynamic reallocation process can insure that colleges and universities are able to meet the challenges and opportunities of the future.

We appreciate the cooperation of the institutions that participated in the study; this willingness to share experiences demonstrates the best in American higher education.

D.F. Finn
Senior Vice President

Acknowledgments

NACUBO's Financial Management Committee supervised the development of this monograph. Committee members are:

A.W. Flowers (Chairman)
Executive Vice Chancellor
Maricopa County Community
  College Systems Office

David J. Berg
Director of Management Planning
  and Information Services
University of Minnesota

Jack C. Blanton
Vice Chancellor for Administration
University of Kentucky

James Grant
Vice President for Administration
SUNY College at New Paltz

Robert E. Kirkpatrick
Vice President for Business Affairs
New Mexico State University

Burton Sonenstein
Vice President for Administration
  and Finance and Treasurer
Wesleyan University

George L. Worsley
Vice Chancellor for Finance
  and Business
North Carolina State University

Dennis Jones (ex-officio)
Vice President for
  Planning and Evaluation
National Center for Higher
  Education Management Systems

The project director and principal author of the monograph was James A. Hyatt, director of the Financial Management Center. Co-authors were Carol Herrnstadt Shulman and Aurora A. Santiago.

Case studies were based on site visits to and documents provided by five public institutions in three states that experienced severe reductions in state appropriations. The Financial Management Committee would like to express special appreciation to the following resource persons at the respective institutions for their cooperation in the project.

University of Washington

James F. Ryan
Vice President of Business and
Finance

Robert K. Thompson
Vice Provost for Planning and
Budgeting

University of Idaho

David McKinney
Financial Vice President

Jerry Wallace
Budget Director

Michigan State University

Kenneth W. Thompson
Vice President for Finance and
Operations and Treasurer

Robert Lockhart
Director, Office of Planning and
Budgets

University of Michigan—Ann Arbor

James F. Brinkerhoff
Vice President and Chief Financial
Officer

Robert W. Moenart
Director, Office of Financial Analysis

R. Sue Mims
Director, Office of Academic
Planning and Analysis

Seattle Community College District

Donald G. Phelps
Chancellor

James Christiansen
Vice Chancellor for Business
and Finance

John W. Casey
President (former Chancellor of
the District)
Pasadena City College

The field review edition of the monograph was sent to a number of college and university business officers and other knowledgeable persons. The Financial Management Committee and project staff express appreciation to these reviewers, whose comments and suggestions were used in revising the study. In particular, they recognize the contribution of William Vandament, of the California State University and Colleges System Office, in the critique and revision of this book. The committee and staff also acknowledge the support and assistance provided by D.F. Finn of NACUBO.

Preface

To meet the need for information on reallocation, NACUBO conducted a study of retrenchment and reallocation processes at five public colleges and universities: the University of Washington, University of Idaho, University of Michigan, Michigan State University, and Seattle Community College District. These institutions are located in three of the states that have been hit hardest by revenue shortfalls. As a result, the NACUBO study highlights efforts by institutions under severe political, economic, and time pressure.

At each institution visited, project staff met with key administrators in both academic and support areas, as well as with faculty members and students who had been involved in retrenchment and reallocation activities.

The initial intent of the NACUBO study was to examine the effects of revenue reductions on colleges and universities and to document ways in which these institutions responded to fiscal stress. In this regard, the study focused first on retrenchment or how institutions reduced expenditures and curtailed operations. However, as project staff visited each institution, it became clear that while retrenchment was common during initial reductions, the long-term approach to fiscal stress was reallocation, or "a process which redistributes resources according to a plan." Therefore, the focus of this book has been expanded to include the broader process of reallocation, which is critical to continued viability of institutions under fiscal stress.

The book consists of two parts: (1) an overview of institutional approaches to retrenchment and reallocation, and (2) five individual case studies that highlight institutional approaches to retrenchment and reallocation. When reviewing these studies, note that the process developed by a particular college or university is largely determined by internal and external factors impinging on that institution. Thus, while experiences of the institutions studied can provide valuable guidance for other colleges and universities, it is incumbent on each institution to develop a reallocation plan that addresses its particular role and mission.

Reallocation and Retrenchment: Responses to Fiscal Stress

This chapter provides an overview of two aspects of institutional responses to fiscal stress. First, it presents factors that influence institutional responses of reallocation and retrenchment; such factors include duration of the fiscal crisis, degree of management flexibility available to the institution, and diversification of institutional revenue sources.

Second, important components of effective reallocation are described. In developing an effective reallocation process, for example, an institution must consider such elements as faculty and constituent involvement in the process, ability of an institution to reformulate its role and mission, and need to maintain and/or enhance the quality of academic and support programs. Finally, throughout both retrenchment and reallocation processes, institutions must assess short-term versus long-term costs and benefits associated with these processes.

Determining Approaches to Reallocation

The manner in which an institution approaches reallocation is determined by various internal and external factors. Among these are:

1. Duration of the fiscal crisis.

2. Degree of management flexibility available to the institution.

3. Diversification of institutional revenue sources.

4. Historical level of recurring program support.

5. Ability of administration to communicate with all the institution's constituent groups.

The significance of these factors in shaping reallocation processes at the institutions studied is described below.

1

Duration of the Fiscal Crisis

An institution's response to fiscal stress is often determined by duration of the fiscal crisis. In particular, three factors that shape this response are: (1) short- or long-term nature of the crisis; (2) timing of the budget reductions; and (3) the institution's state of preparedness.

Short- versus Long-Term Crisis. When initially faced with a reduction, an institution normally assesses the duration of the crisis. If the situation appears to be for a short term, across-the-board reductions usually are instituted in all programs. Such actions include reduction or deferral in support services, such as plant operation and maintenance; travel freezes; deferral of equipment purchases; and hiring freezes. If the fiscal crisis worsens, a mixture of across-the-board and selective program reductions are implemented. Largest reductions normally are made in noninstructional areas and in academic programs not central to main instructional and/or research purposes of the institution, for example, certain public services and ancillary activities. In addition, where possible, there is an attempt to make certain activities self-supporting, such as public radio and television operations, continuing education programs, and some institutional services. If possible, tuition and fees are raised to generate additional revenue. As hope of an early solution to the fiscal crisis diminishes, institutions implement major program reductions. At the University of Washington, University of Michigan, and Michigan State University, these reductions were targeted through an institution-wide program review process, in which the focus was not only budget reduction but also resource reallocation.

Timing of Budget Reductions. Frequently, budget reductions occur during the academic year. Both Michigan State University and the University of Michigan were well into the fiscal year when they received an appropriation that was significantly below budgeted levels. In order to respond, these institutions implemented a number of one-time measures. Michigan State University, for example, imposed a $20 registration fee surcharge for the winter and spring terms and laid off all but essential personnel for two and one-half days. In addition, many special projects were deferred.

The effects of midperiod budget reductions are often magnified since a 5% reduction in midyear usually represents a 10% or more reduction of remaining unexpended funds. In addition, far fewer options are available for reducing expenditures if a budget cut occurs during the academic year. Since colleges and universities are labor-intensive, budgets are difficult to alter on a short-term basis. Contracts with students and faculty, for example, must be honored. As a result, it has been estimated that less than half of an institution's projected expenditures are subject to reduction once a fiscal year has begun.

State of Preparedness. A state of preparedness exists at an institution if one or more of the following actions have been taken prior to the fiscal crisis. First, contingency funds have been established to deal temporarily with revenue shortfalls. In the words of Harold Shapiro, president of the University of Michigan, this means "the conventional and prudent practice of maintaining sufficient financial liquidity so that if revenues fall, or expenditures unexpectedly increase, monies can be found to fill the gap." Second, efforts have been made to reduce ongoing contractual commitments with faculty and staff. In this regard, Michigan State University's special retirement options and intra-university transfers represent an excellent approach to faculty and staff reductions.

Third, a state of preparedness exists when reviews of an institution's role, mission, and programs are part of an ongoing management process. Review processes, such as the University of Washington's "university review process," enable administrators to make informed and responsible reallocation decisions. These reviews enable the institution to identify areas in which long-term reductions or reallocations may be necessary. For such review and sound institutional planning, adequate institutional data bases are essential.

Financial Management Flexibility

Flexibility in financial management is another critical element in determining an institution's response to fiscal stress. Ability to carry forward funds from one fiscal year to the next, for example, can allow an institution to build reserves gradually and systematically and be in a better position to respond to fiscal crisis. Ability to establish reserves, however, should be exercised carefully since existence of such reserves may provide an excellent rationale for further reductions in state support of a public institution's base budget.

Another element of financial flexibility is the ability of an institution to transfer funds among budgetary units and between expenditure categories. The University of Idaho, for example, found that such flexibility enabled it to respond more effectively to budget reductions and permitted it to minimize the impact of reductions on key institutional areas, such as libraries and student services. It should also be noted that benefits derived from such actions can be increased if flexibility is applied not only centrally but also at college and departmental levels.

Some institutions studied, Michigan State University in particular, made judicious use of cash management techniques in responding to budget reductions. Position control systems and central capture of salaries from vacant faculty and staff positions are two methods of obtaining funds to offset revenue shortfalls. Some institutions also achieved cost reductions by consolidating or merging existing offices or programs.

Cost saving can also be achieved by investing funds in the upgrading of management processes and procedures. The University of Idaho, for example, has improved its internal budget management procedures through innovative use of computer technology. Similarly, Seattle Community College has made effective use of an automated library reference system—the Washington Library Network—to improve library operation.

Diversification of Revenue Sources

A diversification of revenue sources is helpful in avoiding major dislocations caused by drastic funding reductions. Because of the diversity and composition of its funding sources, the University of Michigan, for example, has had more flexibility in responding to budget reductions than institutions that are totally dependent on state appropriations. In addition, if a college or university is able to set tuition and fee levels, it may partially offset losses in state support by increasing tuition and fee revenues. This option was available to the University of Michigan and Michigan State University but not to the University of Washington or the University of Idaho, whose tuition levels are set at the state level.

In order to diversify their revenue sources, certain institutions increased their development activities. At Michigan State, for example, the commitment of funds to a number of small capital campaigns enabled the university to raise $9 million. In addition, other institutions, such as the University of Michigan, are seeking to strengthen their ties with business and industry.

Historical Level of Recurring Program Support

An institution's historical level of recurring program support is a major factor in determining its approach to retrenchment or reallocation. New institutions or those with a recent history of budget reductions have fewer financial options in responding to retrenchment. Michigan State University, for example, grew rapidly during the 1960s and 1970s. In the process, it greatly expanded the scope and depth of its program offerings by adding departments, colleges, and professional schools. By the 1980s, however, state support for higher education had declined. In approaching reallocation the board of trustees thus noted:

> The one option we do not have is to recommend minimal changes or no changes. . . .the decision problem we face is radically different. Our decision problem is which programs should be sustained and which should be

curtailed or eliminated. Michigan State cannot be all things to all people. In fact, the University is not funded at a level which will allow it to continue all its current programs. (*Coordinated Proposals*, 1981.)

Recognizing this, Michigan State University has been guided by a fundamental consideration in reallocation: all programs and activities must be examined in terms of their centrality to the university's role and mission.

Effective Communication with Constituent Groups

A final factor that influences reallocation is the administration's ability to communicate with all institutional constituents. An adequate dialogue should be maintained not only with students, faculty, and staff but also with alumni, the general public, and leaders in business and industry. It is essential that these groups are informed of reasons for reallocation and the options available to them. In this regard, administrators should pursue a middle course between dramatic predictions of doom and a low-key approach which understates the real impact of reductions on the institution. As evidenced by experiences of the institutions studied, an informed faculty, staff, and student body help to insure the success of reallocation.

Developing a Reallocation Process

Important elements to consider in developing an effective reallocation process include:

1. Faculty and constituent involvement in reallocation.

2. Assessment of institutional role and mission.

3. Quality of academic and support programs.

4. Long-term versus short-term costs and benefits associated with reallocation.

Faculty and Constituent Involvement in Reallocation

To be successful, the reallocation process should have the active involvement of faculty, students, and other constituent groups. At a majority of the institutions studied, a steering committee composed of senior administrators, faculty, and students was established to guide reallocation. At the University of Michigan, this body was the budget priorities committee; at the University of Washington, an ad hoc planning group which included the provost, vice president for health sciences, dean of the graduate school, and chairman of the faculty senate's council on planning and priorities.

Most institutions visited found that level and quality of communica-tion among all staff improved during the reallocation process. Once the need and rationale for reallocation were explained, faculty and staff, and particularly academic and financial administrators, cooperated to make the process work.

Assessment of Institutional Role and Mission

A thorough understanding of an institution's role and mission is the foundation on which a successful reallocation process must be built. A program review process that is conducted within the context of institu-tional role and mission helps to identify high priority areas and those in which programs should be reduced or eliminated and resources reallocated. In 1983, for example, administrators at Michigan State University declared:

> Maintaining academic excellence in the midst of changing financial condi-tions demands constant attention to the university's mission and goals and requires a continuous process of universitywide strategic planning.

The University of Michigan referred to its role and mission statement in identifying six programmatic (rather than organizational) areas as beneficiaries of reallocation:

- Faculty and staff salaries.

- Research, including generating better incentives for research.

- Undergraduate teaching and incentives for better teaching.

- An improved level of merit-based support for graduate students.

- Funds to regenerate the budgetary capacity to respond to new intellectual developments and social needs and to provide for selected program growth and development.

- An improved level of support for instructional and research equipment and renovation of physical facilities.

Quality of Academic and Support Programs

A concern for maintaining or enhancing institutional quality underlies most reallocation plans. While measuring quality remains a difficult task, program reviews combined with input from other sources, such as accreditation reports, help to identify strong and weak areas of an institution. At the University of Washington, for example, the quality of faculty and of graduate programs has been of major concern. As a consequence, salary merit pools have not been used to offset reduced support; rather, they continue to be used for their intended purpose, in the belief that high-quality faculty must be rewarded. Also, no reductions have been made in the graduate research fund.

Long-term versus Short-term Costs and Benefits Associated with Reallocation

In developing reallocation processes, administrators must be sensitive to both the short- and long-term implications of their actions.

Reduction in support units. While support areas are often among the first targets for retrenchment or reallocation, reductions in these areas may have negative long-term effects on an institution. For example, an institution's inability to comply with state reporting or audit requirements can adversely affect the institution's reputation with the state and other funding sources. As a consequence, such a loss of institutional credibility may mean that funds allocated to the institution will be further reduced. Similarly, reductions in student services can impair an institution's ability to attract and retain high-quality students, faculty, and staff. Quality of instruction and research programs can also be adversely affected by inadequate support.

When considering reductions in the support area, administrators should be aware that false economies may result when reductions in departmental support merely result in increased demand for central support services, such as accounting and purchasing.

Deferring equipment purchases. Deferral of equipment purchases can provide some relief from short-term budget reductions. In the long run, however, inadequate funding of equipment can lead to serious erosion of the capacity and quality of instruction and research programs. Inadequate facilities and equipment can also impair the institution's ability to attract research grants and contracts.

Reductions in library services. Availability of adequate library services is critical to the instructional and/or research mission of an institution. Reductions in breadth and diversity of a library's collections, in its hours of operation, and in its range of services can seriously impair the institution's ability to provide adequate support to instructional and research programs and its ability to attract and retain high-quality students, faculty, and staff. As a result, what appears to be a short-term solution to budget cuts can result in major long-term problems.

Deferral of plant maintenance. Deferring plant maintenance can have long-term implications for the institution's academic programs. If programs cannot be adequately housed or if library collections and research equipment cannot be adequately protected, the institution runs the risk of undermining its instructional and research capacity. In addition, deteriorating facilities and equipment expose the institution to potential legal liabilities resulting from accidents and/or injuries. It is important to note that such liabilities might offset savings from cost reductions in this area.

Conclusion

A fundamental question emerges from the previous discussion: are institutions improved by going through retrenchment and/or realloca-tion? Concerning reallocation, the experiences of the institutions studied are generally positive. A planning document from the University of Washington, for example, states that:

> A university can contract in size and scope without losing its claim to excellence. If choices facing it are made well, based on carefully developed plans, excellence need not suffer. Some activities of the university may be reduced in scope; others may be eliminated as the university carefully restricts its range of offerings. The result, it is hoped, will be an institution of excellence ready to meet the challenges of the next century on a stable and predictable financial foundation. (*Long-Range Problems, Desires, and Priorities*, 1982.)

Other institutions currently involved in reallocation have found that this process has improved faculty and staff understanding of the institu-tion's role and mission and has helped in setting institutional priorities. Reallocation has also prompted an in-depth discussion of the long- and short-term implications associated with alternative decisions.

It is imperative that the institutional administration understand the process of resource reallocation and be aware of alternative processes for implementing it at their institutions. If colleges and universities are to meet the challenges facing them in the years ahead, reallocation must be made an integral part of institutional management.

The University of Washington

A university can contract in size or scope without losing its claim to excellence.

Only two years after he had become president of the University of
Washington, William P. Gerberding was forced to revise his assumptions about the institution's future. As a new president in summer 1979,
Gerberding launched an academic program and fiscal review process to
become familiar with institutional operations and plan for future
development. The University of Washington's prognosis was for
growth, not for retrenchment and reallocation. However, changes in the
state's economic outlook between 1980 and 1982 forced major budget
cuts at the university.

Institutional Profile

President Gerberding's optimistic view was linked to the state's
prospering economy in the late seventies. Under state policy, the legislature has full control over public institutions' revenues. The legislature
sets tuition and fees, and institutions deposit this income in the state
general fund, so there is no relationship between tuition revenue and
state appropriations to colleges and universities. Furthermore, state
policy requires that increases in local income be considered offsets to the
general fund appropriation.

As a result, the university does not control its tuition and fees nor
does it benefit from other sources of revenue that flow directly into the
state's general fund. The university is thus restricted in managing short-
range financial emergencies and subject to unpredictable and immediate
budget reductions when state revenues fail to meet anticipated levels of
income. This situation is exacerbated when the state does not carry
"rainy-day" reserves. Moreover, as a result of legislative actions in 1981
and 1982, the university's capital budget and operating budget are in
direct competition with one another, each being heavily dependent on
the same general fund revenue base. (Previously, sources of capital
revenue were used for operating purposes to augment state general fund
operating appropriations.)

Academically, the University of Washington is a leading research
institution, ranking fourth in the nation in amount of federal funds
received and first among public universities. It has relied on grants and
contracts for the last several years to maintain its research position.
During 1982, total income from grants and contracts surpassed state
support for the university. In 1980–81, grant and contract income
totaled $162.9 million; in 1981–82, it increased slightly to $163.3 million
and in 1982–83 stood at $171.3 million. On the other hand, state
general fund tax support was $172.4 million; $138.3 million if tuition and
fee deposits to the general funds are excluded.

Graduate students in Masters and Ph.D. programs accounted for 22% of total enrollment, or 7,710 in 1981. Enrollments in professional schools—medicine, dentistry, and law—account for 4% of the student body, but have grown by 33% over the decade.

On the undergraduate level, headcount enrollment in fall 1979 was just over 24,000. Demand for admission to the university is high and long-range plans formulated in 1982 project a stable fall headcount enrollment of 35,250, resulting in an FTE enrollment of 31,000 for each academic year through 1987. Given the state of Washington's economy, this projection may be overly optimistic. The operating budget request assumes a carry-forward budget adequate for an average annual enroll-ment of 28,500 FTE students, and seeks additional funding of $12.3 million to accommodate a higher average annual enrollment of 30,000 FTE students. It is likely that the university's 1983–85 FTE enrollment will be 29,500 FTE, significantly lower than 31,000.

Between 1980 and 1982, this information and more was subjected to an intensive review. Support services, academic programs, long-term goals, and institutional mission were scrutinized. As the state economy went rapidly downhill, the university was forced to consider all these aspects of institutional activities in making reductions.

Chronology

The University of Washington's turnabout in expectations over a two-year period parallels the experiences of Washington state during the same time. University reallocation and retrenchment were caused in large part by overoptimistic state budgetary actions.

Washington state's economic outlook was good in the summer of 1979. It had experienced population and economic growth unparalleled in its history and significantly greater than that of the country as a whole during the late seventies. The state legislature thus began the 1979–81 biennium by spending generously. It obligated all of its current revenues anticipated from continued economic growth and nearly all the surplus accumulated to that point to fund current programs and to start new ones.

However, as the state's economy declined, the governor and legislature were required by law to keep expenditures in line with pro-jected revenues. Consequently, a flurry of state actions resulted in budget cuts in all state agencies, to which the University of Washington was no exception.

The 1979–81 state appropriation for the university was $378.5 million (in 1981–83 dollars), including tuition and fees of $47 million and a capital fund balance diversion of $21.3 million. The net state tax appropriation was $310.2 million. In July 1981, the new appropriation was $384.8 million, including $70.6 million from tuition and fees and a $55.4 million capital fund balance diversion, a net state tax appropriation of $258.8 million. The university was subjected to three more reductions, resulting in a total appropriation of $348.9 million by July 1982 for the 1981–83 biennium, including $73.3 million from tuition and fees and a $48.3 million capital fund diversion, a net tax appropriation of $223.3 million. These figures demonstrate that the University of Washington was significantly affected by state economic problems—absolute state budget reductions of $33.6 million, state use of the university's capital fund balances ($48.3 million), and significant increases in student tuition and fees ($26.2 million in constant dollars).

This case study chronicles how the university responded to its inclusion in Washington state's budgetary whirlwind. Table I shows the chronology of events.

Table I

Chronology

Date	Action
April 1980 (1979–81 biennium)	Budget cuts ordered equal to 3% of second year budget ($4.7 million). Selective and differential reductions made in noninstructional support services, and public service and ancillary activities.
Summer 1980	State agencies ordered to submit target budgets that are 12% below existing carry-forward budgets for 1981–83 biennium. Formal review process—the "university review"—begun.
October 1980	Additional budget cut ordered equal to 2% of second-year budget. Across-the-board reductions occur, pending completion of university review.
April 1981	Legislature enacts 1981–83 budget approximately equal to previous biennium budget, less budget reductions already taken ($7.8 million shortfall of amount needed for 1979–81 budget, given built-in escalator factors).
	Legislature also mandates a 70% increase in tuition and fees over next two years, money being deposited in state general fund.
	Selective cuts made to compensate for shortfall.

September 1981   State agencies ordered to begin cutting 1981–83 general fund budgets by 10.1%, a total of $32 million at the university.

Board of regents, at president's request, declares a state of financial emergency.

November–   Special legislative session passes revenue adjustments, reducing university's cut to 5.5%, or $17 million. Declaration of state of financial emergency rescinded. Selective and across-the-board cuts made, largely in support services (student services, administrative services, and physical plant).
December 1981

April 1982   Legislature passes new revenue measures, but reduces state programs further. A 2.2% reduction, totaling $6 million, taken in one-time reductions.

July 1982   Legislature enacts new revenue measures, reduces university's budget by another 2.2%, or more than $7 million. One-time reductions made.

Fall 1982   Three- to four-year plan developed to effect permanent savings of $13 million, taken on a temporary basis in April and July.

1983–85 budget request reflects $38.5 million (12%) budget reductions from 1980–82.

Approaches to Reallocation and Retrenchment

In a review of the university's activities from 1980 to 1982, it was stated in an institutional planning document that:

> A university can contract in size or scope without losing its claim to excellence. If the choices facing it are made well, based on carefully developed plans, excellence need not suffer. Some activities of the university may be reduced in scope; others may be eliminated as the university carefully restricts its range of offerings. The result, it is hoped, will be an institution of excellence ready to meet the challenges of the next century on a stable and predictable financial foundation. (*Long-range Problems, Desires and Priorities,* 1982)

To attain this goal, the university took three courses of action: (1) institutionwide review of programs and support services, (2) cuts in support services, and (3) retrenchment and reallocation in academic programs.

Review Processes

It is generally believed that institutional program reviews should guide retrenchment and reallocation processes. Such reviews can help institutions decide what is essential to their role, mission, and institutional quality, and consequently what can be discarded or reallocated under severe financial constraints.

The University of Washington used two internal review processes to decide where it could reduce support services and academic programs. The university already had review processes in operation when the budgetary axe first fell, and it initiated an even more comprehensive review once it became apparent that further cuts would be necessary. As results of this second review became available, reductions began to be more selective rather than across-the-board.

President Gerberding initiated the first review after he came to the campus in summer 1979. A series of overall academic program reviews were conducted with each dean to acquaint the new president with operations of the university's major colleges and schools, including problems, strengths, and goals. In addition, all administrative units participated in a modified zero base budget review process in order to: (1) identify their respective administrative support activities, personnel associated with these activities, and rationale for the activity (mandatory, required, necessary, or useful); and (2) assess program efficiency and effectiveness. These review processes were used to respond on a differential basis to the first budget cut of 3% ordered in April 1980.*

The second review process—the university review—was launched after the governor ordered the university to submit a target budget that was 12% below the carry-forward budget for the 1981–83 biennium. This order underscored the university's need to plan for potential budget cuts and to develop long-range plans that keyed university programs to diminished financial resources. The university review provided the rationale which would be used to make later decisions on budget cuts. It also provided an orderly planning document on which the university community could rely during the more unpredictable process of state-mandated cuts.

---

*Furthermore, all graduate programs are reviewed regularly, and the results are made available to deans and departments for use in program and resource planning and in budget allocation decisions. These reports are reviewed by the central administration as well as by deans, chairpersons, and departmental faculty.

The first stage of the university review was initiated during the 1980–81 academic year. The faculty senate developed criteria that academic units would use to review their programs; deans and vice presidents submitted unit self-assessments; and faculty task forces, appointed by the provost, evaluated review documents which had been prepared by both academic support and institutional support units.

In the 1981–82 academic year, the university review was continued in an atmosphere of financial crisis. State revenues declined precipitously, a situation that forced the governor to estimate that the university's operating budget would have to be cut by an additional $32.1 million (10.1%). Faced with that prospect, the board of regents, on the recommendation of President Gerberding and the faculty senate leadership, declared a state of financial emergency. As a result of the regents' action, the university administration, in consultation with the faculty senate's financial emergency committee, proceeded to plan for a 10.1% reduction. Because of its size, such a reduction required that the university review also include reduction and elimination of academic programs.

For a time, university efforts focused on this new crisis. Legislative actions in November 1981 ameliorated the situation, reducing the ordered 10.1% cut to 5.5%.

In December 1981, the board of regents declared an end to the state of financial emergency on the advice of President Gerberding and the financial emergency committee. The 5.5% reduction was implemented on the basis of program and budget reviews conducted in preparing for the 10.1% reduction. The reduction had a heavy impact on public service and ancillary support services (differentially) and on central administrative services and physical plant operation and maintenance. Once the 5.5% cuts were in place, the university turned its attention to completing the university review.

In February 1982, the provost established an ad hoc planning group to assist him in identifying and developing issues that would appropriately guide university planning. As the provost explained in a letter to the academic deans, dated February 4, 1982:

> The Ad Hoc Planning Group will assist me in formulating a first draft University Review document for subsequent discussion with the board of deans and the faculty senate. To assist us in drafting this document, the Ad Hoc Planning Group will meet with individual deans to review their long-range plans. Because the University Review materials, submitted by colleges and schools in the spring of 1981, varied considerably in depth, coverage of issues, and presentation, the Ad Hoc Planning Group formulated a series of principles and questions it believed would help the

university and its colleges and schools address long-range planning. The principles and questions were derived from the University Review materials, the criteria for academic program review formulated by the faculty senate, and the plans which were under discussion during the state of financial emergency.

This ad hoc planning group included the provost, vice president for health sciences, dean and associate dean of the Graduate School, dean of the College of Arts and Sciences, and chairperson of the faculty senate's council on planning and priorities. The group was assisted by the vice provost for planning and budgeting and members of his staff.

The planning group met with each dean during February and March 1982. Subsequently, each dean submitted a written report based on university review questions and any additional issues that arose. After meeting with deans, the planning group identified major long-range planning issues that emerged from written reports and formulated preliminary plans for addressing them.

Equally concerned about these issues, the faculty senate executive committee established an ad hoc task force on long-range planning to set forth the faculty perspective on planning issues. The task force was appointed in April 1982 with the charge "to re-examine the fundamental assumptions of higher education, particularly as they relate to the university." The task force consisted of seven faculty members chosen from various departments in the College of Arts and Sciences and professional schools and colleges, with the chairperson and vice-chairperson of the faculty senate as ex-officio members. Four members of the group were to be appointed by the senate chairperson to serve on the "merged task force," which would write the university planning report.

The ad hoc task force met during April and May, 1982, dividing its work among various subcommittees. In the report submitted to the senate executive committee on May 14, 1982, the task force identified issues and fundamental assumptions concerning the university's role and mission, organization, structure, functions, and educational tasks. The report was submitted to the faculty senate and endorsed in principle as a planning guide on May 20, 1982.

With these two reports in hand, the provost and the faculty senate chairperson appointed a university task force on long-range planning to develop a single, final university review report. This report was drafted over the summer of 1982 and reviewed in the fall by deans, vice presidents, faculty leaders, and administrators. The final report was published on November 15, 1982, and distributed to all faculty and other interested parties.

Reductions in Support Services

During periods of retrenchment, support services frequently are first to experience reduction and those at the University of Washington were no exception. Both institutional and academic support services bore the brunt of budget cuts. Staff losses were high. By fall 1982, a planning document concluded:

> One of the egregious liabilities of recent underfunding has been the general inadequacy of support to university programs. Instructional and research quality have clearly been impaired by the lack of support funding, and the inadequacy has been felt more severely in some areas than others. Once a determination is reached as to which programs the university shall continue to offer, these programs must be provided significantly improved support funding.

The university faced its first budget reduction in April 1980, and the central administration relied on President Gerberding's initial campus review to decide where cuts would occur. Largest reductions were made in noninstructional support services and in ancillary academic programs that were not considered essential to continued functioning of the university (certain public services and support activities). Support services were further cut in October 1980 when the university levied an across-the-board cut of 2% in response to new state orders, and pending conclusion of the university review.

But the biggest blow to support services followed the order to reduce the university budget by 5.5% or $17 million in December 1981 (as opposed to the threatened 10.1% cut). Following intensive communitywide discussion of university review documents, the administration first focused on centrally directed selective reductions in areas such as public services, student services, administrative functions, physical plant-related functions, and other ancillary support services. Once these selective reductions had been identified, efforts were made to cut as much as possible from support units. Target reductions were sent to all nonacademic support units; the latter were asked to indicate plans for making such reductions and the anticipated impact of these reductions not only on directly affected units, but also on academic programs, other campus units, and the university's ability to function effectively in the long run. After these cuts were made, remaining reductions occurred in academic units based on the university review. Table II summarizes these cuts.

Table II

University of Washington
1981–83 Biennium Carry-forward Budget Reduction Summary
($000's)

| | | Biennial Carry-forward Reductions | | | |
| | *Biennial Carry-forward Reduction Base[1]* | *December 1981 Reduction* | *October 1982 Reduction* | *Total* | *%* |
Program					
01 Instruction	212,577	5,692	11,800	17,492	8.2%
02 Research	4,247	262	—	262	6.2%
03 Public Service	1,381	307	—	307	22.2%
04 Primary Support Services	21,994	1,881	—	1,881	8.6%
Total Academic Programs	240,199	8,142	11,800	19,942	8.3%
05 Libraries	23,909	1,475	8	1,483	6.2%
06 Student Services	12,433	2,680[2]	108	2,788[3]	22.4%
07 Hospitals Academic Support	27,026	1,537	204	1,741	6.4%
08 Institutional Support	38,703	3,116	432	3,548	9.2%
09 Plant Operation and Maintenance	48,703	4,808	528	5,336	11.0%
Total	390,973	21,758	13,080	34,838	8.9%

---

[1]Beginning level carry-forward budget net of dedicated income and indirect cost revenue.
[2]Net real reduction of $1,036,000 given income offset of $1,644,000.
[3]Net real reduction of $1,144,000 or 9.2% given income offset of $1,644,000.

Business and Financial Services

Effects of cuts in business and finance between July 1979 (before cuts were made) and July 1982 are shown in Table III.

Largest decreases in number of staff FTEs were sustained in business and plant services and in personnel services; these decreases were 168.74 and 6.39, respectively.

Table III

Organizational Element	Authorized FTE July 1, 1979	Authorized FTE July 1, 1982	FTE Decrease	Percent Decrease
Vice President	6.50	4.75	1.75	27%
Administrative Data Processing	105.80	105.30	.50	—
Business and Plant Services	1,069.63	900.89	168.74	16%
Financial Services	176.85	172.87	3.98	2%
Internal Audit	7.58	7.58	—	—
Personnel Services	78.04	71.65	6.39	8%
Total Business & Finance	1,444.40	1263.04	181.36	13%

For the biennium 1981–83, total reductions in institutional support amounted to $3,548,000, or 9.2% of the budget.

Custodial Services. The hardest-hit unit within business and finance was the custodial program. It lost 42 positions between July 1980 and November 1982. Consequently, the ratio of building area served per FTE custodian rose from 29,000 square feet to almost 35,000 during this period, a 20% increase. Because health codes require daily cleaning of restrooms and public areas, the overload was assigned to classroom and private office cleaning. Window washing was eliminated from the budget, but because of complaints, is now done on a recharge basis in some areas.

Police. Budget reductions resulted in a loss of 25 permanent FTE positions in the police department. As a result, there is one less officer per shift on average. Regular foot patrols were replaced by sporadic building checks. Security services for special facilities (such as an art gallery) are now contracted out to a private company.

Audit. In the audit department, even the loss of two new unfilled staff positions was critical, particularly since new concerns had developed about fiscal integrity. As funding levels declined, campus departments sought new and creative methods of generating income. Reductions in departments' administrative staff support decreased their capabilities to monitor their operations adequately. Many departments sought assistance from the understaffed audit department; however, the internal audit workload increased substantially because of additional externally mandated audit requirements and the formation of new campus recharge centers. Furthermore, audits totaling 270 days were deferred for 1982.

Academic Support

In academic support, university libraries were protected, but still lost nearly $1.5 million. According to a university planning document, this substantial reduction has meant that:

> A significant number of titles that would otherwise have been acquired will not be available on the campus; titles that can be purchased take longer to appear in the card catalogs; it is more difficult to use the libraries' collections because many of the units are open fewer hours; it is also more difficult to use the collections because not only are there fewer staff to provide all levels of assistance, but the libraries' program of providing instructional services that result in users being better able to help themselves has been drastically reduced; finally, it is no longer possible to attract and retain the top-quality staff that is essential to the libraries and is, thus, essential to the university's programs.

Total reduction for libraries during the 1981–83 biennium was $1,483,000, or 6.2% of the budget.

With regard to instructional support, severe limitations were imposed on clerical and scientific staffing, supplies and materials, and travel and contracted services. According to testimony from both faculty and administrators, these deficiencies had a serious impact on the quality of instruction. Lack of instructional support and salary deterioration were major causes for loss of faculty and staff, who went to more favorable employment elsewhere.

Equipment funds also sustained major budget reductions. Efforts to correct equipment deficiencies almost ceased during the 1981–83 biennium, when the equipment component in the operating budget was eliminated. Although $6.8 million was provided for equipment in the capital budget, continuing budget reductions and capital revenue shortfalls because of decline in timber sales on university lands have virtually eliminated equipment replacement.

Total reduction for primary support services during 1981–83 was $1,881,000 or 8.6% of the budget.

Reductions in Student Services

Student services sustained a reduction of five FTE staff. Conse-quently, remaining staff assumed additional duties, causing students to wait longer for service and increasing their general frustration with the system. Moreover, other university units now must provide information and assistance for which they previously relied on the student affairs office.

Overall, significant cuts in support services have adversely affected staff morale. Staff have been laid off, workload has increased, and, most important, those who continue to work in these areas see the business of the university falling farther and farther behind.

The total reduction for student services was $2,788,000, or 22.4% of the budget, during the 1981–83 biennium.

Effects of Retrenchment
on Academic Programs and Faculty

Academic programs and faculty are at the heart of a college or univer-sity and are key to implementing the institution's role and mission. Thus, during the onslaught of budget cuts between 1980 and 1982, academic programs became subject to cutbacks only after support services were reduced, and suffered comparatively less. Nevertheless, budget cuts were not insignificant. Reduction in academic programs catalyzed a thorough re-evaluation of unit contributions to the essential role and mission of the university and forced departments and schools to re-examine and, in some cases, to redefine their goals.

Following the declaration of financial emergency and subsequent lift-ing of that condition, academic programs were subjected to certain budget cuts in winter 1982. Central administration made cuts on the basis of data developed by deans during the financial emergency. The deans determined reductions for their colleges after receiving final reduc-tion figures (see Table IV).

Cuts in academic programs made instruction less flexible, reduced opportunities to attract new faculty, and increased academic workload. For example, faculty positions were eliminated through attrition, resulting in fewer classes and more multiclass sections. Part-time, temporary, annual, and visiting faculty were reduced. Faculty workload increased, but there was less support staff to assist faculty members.

These reductions were mild, however, compared to the hard decisions that followed in April and June 1982 and ultimately in October of that year. That spring, a series of legislative actions resulted in a $13 million reduction in financial support. The university took certain one-time-only measures to deal with this new crisis, including offering early retirement

Table IV

1981–83 Biennium Carry-Forward Budget Reduction
College and School Summary

	Biennial Carry-Forward Reduction Base*	December 1981 Reduction	%	October 1982 Reduction	%	Total Reduction	%
General University							
Architecture & Urban Planning	4,549,446	(117,736)	(2.6)	(970,000)	(21.3)	(1,087,736)	(23.9)
Arts & Sciences	73,520,110	(1,719,210)	(2.3)	(4,280,000)	(5.8)	(5,999,210)	(8.2)
Business Administration	10,090,220	(159,151)	(1.6)	(826,000)	(8.2)	(985,151)	(9.8)
Education	7,829,547	(641,279)	(8.2)	(1,195,000)	(15.3)	(1,836,279)	(23.5)
Engineering	15,855,246	(88,929)	(0.6)	(522,000)	(3.3)	(610,929)	(3.9)
Forest Resources	3,420,405	(56,588)	(1.6)	—	—	(56,588)	(1.6)
Graduate School/Research	4,717,419	(482,201)	(10.2)	—	—	(482,201)	(10.2)
Law School	4,719,795	(79,843)	(1.7)	—	—	(79,843)	(1.7)
Ocean & Fishery Sciences	6,363,240	(156,519)	(2.5)	—	—	(156,519)	(2.5)
Public Affairs	1,464,703	(170,736)	(11.7)	—	—	(170,736)	(11.7)
Social Work	3,436,258	(190,840)	(5.6)	—	—	(190,840)	(5.6)
Total	135,966,389	(3,863,032)	(2.8)	(7,793,000)	(5.7)	(11,656,032)	(8.6)

Health Sciences

Dentistry	9,370,299	(403,418)	(4.3)	(1,180,000)	(12.6)	(1,583,418)	(16.9)
Medicine	31,078,228	(841,224)	(2.7)	(1,000,000)	(3.2)	(1,841,224)	(5.9)
Nursing	5,166,531	(171,168)	(3.3)	(330,000)	(6.4)	(501,168)	(9.7)
Pharmacy	2,362,688	(41,544)	(1.8)	(193,000)	(8.1)	(234,544)	(9.9)
Public Health & Community Med.	2,301,664	(56,294)	(2.4)	—	—	(56,294)	(2.4)
Health Sciences	2,461,904	(280,656)	(11.4)	—	—	(280,656)	(11.4)
Total	52,741,314	(1,794,304)	(3.4)	(2,703,000)	(5.1)	(4,497,304)	(8.5)
Other College/School Reductions	—	—	—	(840,000)	—	(840,000)	—
Summer Quarter	6,190,766	(863,590)	(13.9)	(464,000)	(7.5)	(1,327,590)	(21.4)
Continuing Education	1,001,804	(456,969)	(45.6)	—	—	(456,969)	(45.6)
Joint Center for Graduate Study	638,960	(30,146)	(4.7)	—	—	(30,146)	(4.7)
Other Academic Programs	1,863,968	(295,132)	(15.8)	—	—	(295,132)	(15.8)
Academic Computing Services	4,825,062	(28,918)	(0.6)	—	—	(28,918)	(0.6)
Fringe Benefits	36,971,206	(810,073)	(2.2)	—	—	(810,073)	(2.2)
Total	240,199,469	(8,142,164)	(3.4)	(11,800,000)	(4.9)	(19,942,164)	(8.3)

*Net of dedicated income and indirect cost revenue.

to faculty and staff and holding positions vacant. However, certain conditions helped to offset the impact of the cuts, including savings from a
faculty and staff hiring freeze ordered by the governor, fuel savings from
a warm winter, and temporary revenue measures such as additional
interest income on invested fund balances.

Plans to save $13 million on a long-range basis developed more slowly.
Through the summer, the central administration, representatives of the
faculty senate and other faculty, and deans discussed how to reduce the
academic program budget even more, based on criteria specified in the
university review. By October 1982, the academic deans had proposed
program reductions and eliminations which, when fully implemented
over the next three or four years, will result in a permanent savings of
$13 million, 11.8 million from academic programs.

Twenty-nine degree programs were identified for elimination, and
went through a formal termination review process. Largest proposed
reductions were in the College of Architecture and Urban Planning, the
School of Education, and the College of Arts and Sciences. Among
those under consideration for elimination were:

Department of Urban Planning. Bachelor's and Doctoral degree
programs.

Department of Architecture. Bachelor's degree program in architecture. Urban planning and architecture degree programs to be replaced
with collegewide programs.

Department of Kinesiology. Bachelor's and Master's degree
programs.

Department of Near Eastern Languages and Literature. Bachelor's
and Master's degree programs.

School of Nutritional Sciences. Bachelor's and Master's degree
programs in nutrition.

Art Education. Bachelor's degree program.

Children's Drama. Master's degree program.

Actual eliminations followed what had been proposed, with the
following exceptions:

Department of Urban Planning. Doctoral program preserved.

Department of Near Eastern Languages and Literature. Both
Bachelor's and Master's degree programs preserved.

School of Nutritional Sciences. Only Bachelor's degree program eliminated; Master's degree program suspended.

Other program eliminations included:

School and Graduate School of Business Administration. Risk and Insurance Program and Urban Development and Real Estate Program, neither of which granted degrees.

College of Engineering. Department of Humanistic Social Studies and Social Management of Technology program; neither one granted degrees.

College of Forest Resources. Bachelor of Science in Forest Resources—Outdoor Recreation emphasis.

College of Education. Bachelor's and Master's degree programs in business education; also, teacher certification program in business education.

Campus administrators and a graduate student leader interviewed in November 1982 were concerned about effects of both budget cuts and the entire reduction process over the preceding two years. Two major issues of concern were access and program quality.

Access to Academic Programs

Demand for admission to the university is high and, according to estimates, will remain so over the next decade and beyond. The university review report identifies preliminary enrollment projections: the long-time plan assumes a total average annual FTE student enrollment of 31,000 for each academic year through 1987, with an annual autumn quarter student head count of 35,250. The plan also assumes that faculty staffing will remain steady in relation to enrollment. Total undergraduate enrollment is expected to remain essentially steady, graduate enrollment to increase slightly, and professional enrollment to decline slightly.

Major changes in undergraduate enrollment by college and school, over 6 years, are projected to be: an increase in engineering majors from approximately 1,600 to 2,065; an increase in business majors from 1,500 to 1,600; and a decline in arts and sciences undergraduates from 20,163 to 19,724. These changes in enrollment patterns among various schools and colleges reflect student enrollment trends as well as a response to pressures from both within and outside the institution for growth in business and technical areas.

In the health sciences division, enrollment declined between fall 1979 and fall 1983, from 3,151 to 2,835. Dentistry declined from 513 to 389; pharmacy from 291 to 221. Nursing enrollments went from 1,022 to 825 over the period. However, public health and community services rose from 209 to 220, and, more important, the School of Medicine actually increased its enrollment from 1,115 to 1,180. The School of Medicine is party to a state compact with Alaska, Montana, and Idaho, which are ranked lowest nationally with regard to numbers of state residents being trained in medicine per 100,000 people. Therefore, current efforts are being sustained despite reductions.

Program Quality Considerations

The dean of the College of Education saw severe cuts as a stimulus to develop new education and research agendas. He reoriented the focus of the college, stressing research over teacher training, and quality over access. Teacher training programs are being sharply reduced, from 650 students to between 240 and 300, and the grade point average for admission has been raised. Graduate student enrollment also will drop, by about 150 students. More technical support, such as word-processing equipment, will be given to productive researchers. At the same time, faculty has been reduced from 80 to 65, with a long-range target of 55–60.

Campus administrators also expressed sensitivity to problems that budgetary reduction causes faculty, noting the need to sustain their morale by maintaining program quality. For example, the vice provost for research, also concurrently dean of the graduate school, has been concerned about the effect of budget cuts on faculty and on the ability to attract talented graduate students. In determining budget cuts, the university has stressed the need to maintain quality of faculty and of graduate programs. Merit pool funds have not been used to offset reduced support on the grounds that it is always important to reward high-quality faculty. Moreover, no cuts were made in the graduate research fund. Tenured faculty were not terminated, and only selective cuts were made.

Summary

The University of Washington was better able to weather midyear budget cuts than were many other institutions because it had institutional review processes to target its reductions. Still, academic programs, support services, faculty morale, and perceptions of institutional quality all suffered in retrenchment. Many believe, however, that the institution has emerged from the crisis with a better understanding of its role and mission, an appreciation of both long- and short-run costs associated with retrenchment, and a positive future outlook.

Two factors in particular are significant to the university's future. The first is grant support. For the last few years, income from federal grants and contracts has been a primary factor in helping the university maintain its status as a leading research institution. Total income from grants and contracts in 1982 exceeded state support for the university. On the whole, support for research is expected to remain relatively strong, although shifts in sources (such as a possible decrease in research and graduate training support from the federal government and an increase in the much smaller source of private funds for research) will have long-range planning implications for the university.

The second crucial factor is the need for greater fiscal autonomy, which would provide a more stable basis for formulating long-range expenditure plans. The University of Washington is one of the least fiscally autonomous of major research universities. In the absence of a greater degree of fiscal autonomy, and with continuation of relatively unpredictable variations in its revenue sources, long-range planning, which is essential to institutional viability, will remain a difficult task.

The university's outlook is best summarized by the following paragraph discussing the 1983–85 budget approved by the legislature:

Viewed in the context of our difficulties over the past several years, the university's operating and capital budgets for the 1983–85 biennium provide some opportunities to strengthen our academic programs and maintain support services at least at minimum effective levels. Consistent with legislative intent, we will be able to meet some of our major equipment needs, including computing, and we will be able to improve undergraduate instruction in a variety of ways. We will also strengthen our research capabilities by allocating to academic units a significant portion of recovered indirect cost funds. We will be able to address our most pressing fire safety, health, and deferred maintenance problems and to meet some academic program requirements for facility modifications. The university as a whole will benefit substantially from these investments. At the same time, we continue to suffer from a number of deficiencies, especially, for example, our inability to improve instructional support, both in terms of staff and operations. We will have to make our case for such support more effectively. Our capital needs for deferred maintenance, minor repairs and program modifications, major renovations and new facilities are substantially greater than our present financial capacity. Here also we will need to look for new solutions and more effective presentations. In brief, we hope this biennium will provide us with much needed stability and that we can begin to rebuild this great institution.

References

"Maintaining Quality Programs During Periods of Fiscal Stress: An Institutional Perspective" by Robert K. Thompson, vice provost for planning and budgeting, University of Washington. Paper prepared for the Eighth Annual Conference on Higher Education, December 1982.

Report of the University of Washington Task Force on Long-Range Planning (November 1982).

The Seattle
Community College District

Seattle Community College is a comprehensive educational system providing an open door to a stimulating educational environment including academic, vocational and continuing education, and community service programs which are responsive to the changing needs of the diverse communities it serves.

The mission statement of Seattle Community College District (SCCD), formulated in 1978, defines its purposes, as expressed in the opening quotation. Clearly, SCCD perceived its role as a community service organization responsive to changing needs of a diverse population.

When Washington state began experiencing economic crises and all state agencies were ordered to reduce their budgets, SCCD tried to preserve its accessibility and its range of services to the local community. It was successful initially, but continued budget reductions ultimately affected its goals of access and program offerings. SCCD finally had to consider redefining its mission in order to live within the constraints of drastically reduced resources.

Institutional Profile

The Seattle Community College District was formed in 1967 as a result of a new act that established a statewide system of community colleges in order to:

- Offer an open door to every citizen, regardless of academic background or experience, at a cost normally within the student's economic means.

- Insure that each community college district should offer thoroughly comprehensive educational, training, and service programs to meet the needs of both communities and students served by combining, with equal emphasis, high standards of excellence in academic transfer courses; realistic and practical courses in occupational education, both graded and ungraded; community services of an educational, cultural, and recreational nature; and adult education.

SCCD started with one campus, Seattle Central Community College (formerly Edison Technical Institute), and expanded to include two more—North Seattle Community College and South Seattle Community College—in 1970. The district is governed by a five-member board of trustees. There is a district administrative office headed by a district president, who is the chief administrative officer. Campus presidents are responsible for their respective institutions.

Since its creation, SCCD has seen tremendous expansion in access and program offerings. From several hundred students at Edison Technical Institute, it grew to 19,000 students by 1977 and to 28,400 by 1980. During the same period, its course offerings increased from vocational and technical programs to more than 180 certificate and degree programs. In fall 1979, 2,595 class sections were offered. At the same time, total headcount faculty numbered 1,118 (with a full-time equivalent faculty of 360); support staff, 412; and administrators, 86.

As to be expected, expenditures also increased. In 1977–78, general operating funds totaled $20.3 million. By 1981–82, these funds had risen to $28.2 million, a 39% increase.

Funding Formulas

Funding formulas play an important part in SCCD's experience with retrenchment. The state of Washington, through the Council on Post-Secondary Education, developed a series of formulas or "standards" for each major, state-supported operating program within higher education. Standards are based on both inter- and intra-state analysis of such factors as student/faculty ratio by discipline, support staff and cost by program or discipline, and average maintenance and operations cost per square foot. These formulas are the basis for submission of all two-year and four-year higher education requests to the state legislature, which considers the operating budget every second year and then decides at what percentage level it wishes to fund higher education. Appropriations resulting from this process are made directly to each four-year institution and as a lump sum for the community college system. The State Board for Community College Education uses basically the same formulas described above to distribute available funds to the twenty-three community college districts.

Although state formulas have not been changed since 1979–80, neither have they been used for allocation purposes since that period. Reductions effected during 1980–83 were implemented on a pro-rata basis (based on amount of appropriation) with no reference to budget models. This procedure has been true both for reductions and for minor increases made available for the 1983–85 biennium. However, the State Board for Community College Education decided that funds for 1985–86 will be allocated on either the current or a revised formula basis, taking into account differential FTE student demand levels among community college districts.

Funding formulas affect access. In FY1971–72, state-funded full-time equivalent enrollments for the entire community college system in the state of Washington were 66,175.** By FY1980–81, FTE enrollments

---

**One FTE equals approximately two headcount students, and 65% of all students are part-time.

for all community colleges had increased to 104,000. By FY 1981–82, however, statewide FTE enrollments had dropped by 15% to 88,000. For SCCD, corresponding enrollments were 10,460 in 1971–72, 15,040 in 1980–81, and 11,996 in 1981–82. Student enrollment for 1981–82 was 20% below that of the previous year.

Chronology

Table I summarizes cutbacks experienced by SCCD.

Table I

Chronology

Date	Action
FY 1980–81	SCCD's state appropriation is reduced first by 3% and then by 2%, for a total of approximately $1.2 million.
FY 1981–82	Appropriation is reduced further by 2%, or approximately $500,000.
September 1981	Governor orders 10.1% reduction for all state agencies, resulting in a $2.4 million cutback for SCCD.
December 1981	Partial restoration of earlier cutback is declared, amounting to $971,000. Amount is adjusted for a $341,000 carryover to FY 1982–83.
FY 1982–83	SCCD experiences two reductions of 2% each, or $544,000 and $541,000 respectively.
	Shortfall of $20 million in state revenues; additional reduction of $350,000 for SCCD.
October 1982	Individual districts are given option of using merit pool funds to partially offset appropriation reductions.
June 1983	New state legislation passed to increase support for community college system.

When Washington state's economy began to falter in FY1980–81 because of an inadequate tax base, depressed timber and housing industries, and an overall decline in national economy, all state agencies were affected. During this period, Seattle Community College District had its appropriation cut twice—first by 3%, for a loss of $690,000, and then by 2%, for a loss of $493,000. The situation did not improve during the next year, which continued to show a clear pattern of declining state revenues. Early in fiscal year 1981–82, SCCD suffered a further 2% reduction of its operating budget, which meant an additional loss of approximately $500,000.

The steadily worsening state revenue picture prompted the governor to declare a state of financial emergency in September 1981. All state agencies were ordered to implement a 10.1% reduction in state general fund expenditures for 1981–83, with contingency plans for a 20% reduction in the event that K-12 schools would be exempted from across-the-board reductions. The total biennial impact of these reductions on SCCD was estimated to be $6,000,000 at 10.1%. The district was completely unprepared for reductions of this magnitude, the general assumption having been that cuts would be more in the order of 4 to 5%. The governor's order did not specifically define the amount of cutback for SCCD, but a general hiring freeze was prescribed.

To cope with reductions, the budget committee of the Washington Association of Community College Presidents (WACCP) considered several alternative methods of allocating funds, based on the traditional formula approach using various assumptions about FTE enrollments. Ultimately, the state board of education adopted an allocation system based proportionately on the 1980–81 dollar allocation of each district. The 10% reduction plan was implemented in 1981, at a loss of $2.4 million for SCCD during FY1981–82.

A partial restoration amounting to $971,000 occurred in December 1981. Since summer, fall, and winter commitments had already been made, districts were allowed to carry over part of the restoration to 1982–83 as an offset against second-year reductions. SCCD designated $341,000 to the carry-over.

Two additional 2% reductions in 1982–83 resulted in losses of $544,000 and $541,000. The latter cutback resulted when the governor vetoed a specific provision of the early retirement bill that limited agencies to filling only half of all vacancies occurring during the bill's effective period. The governor vetoed this section to avoid problems that occur when an agency is not allowed to fill any vacancies. By substituting a budget cut, agencies were allowed to make appropriate management decisions regarding which positions to fill and which positions, whether vacant or not, were least necessary. This allowed agencies to insure staffing in critical areas based on need rather than chance terminations or retirements.

Approaches to Reallocation

Retrenchment in the Seattle Community College District went through four distinct phases: *Phase one,* in which institutional and academic support services were reduced; *Phase two,* in which across-the-board cuts in all categories occurred; *Phase three,* in which continued reductions greatly impaired a number of activities to the extent that the institution's mission suffered; and *Phase four,* in which the institutional mission and the organizational model of SCCD had to be recast.

For the earlier phases, SCCD was guided by five criteria:

1. The institution's proclaimed mission would be maintained.

2. Core full-time tenured faculty would be retained.

3. Access would be provided for as many students as possible.

4. High quality would be maintained throughout the contraction process.

5. Adequate support services, both administrative and classified, would be maintained. (Chancellor John W. Casey, *Managing Contraction*)

Throughout all phases of reduction, SCCD was particularly concerned about maintaining access to its programs and services, a key aspect of the district's institutional mission.

Phase One (FY1980–81)

In the initial round of reductions, Chancellor Casey noted that:

All were surprised at the contraction that would take place before the institution was seriously jeopardized.... We learned that we could still have a viable institution even after taking budget cutbacks. The area most seriously affected was that of access, then support services.

In this phase, reductions occurred in the following order: administrative support, libraries, capital, affirmative action, services to minorities, community services, student personnel services, and instruction.

Phase Two (Fall 1981)

Starting with this phase and throughout those succeeding, it was much more difficult to selectively identify reductions by area, category, or function. It was necessary to implement reductions in all programs, thus affecting virtually all departments and functions. Moreover, the process through which reductions were imposed at the state level made corresponding implementations at the district level particularly difficult. Casey observed:

> Because cuts were not predictable, were of varying degrees of seriousness, and were sometimes made and then retracted, planning in an organized manner was rendered all but impossible.

Among areas targeted for reduction were maintenance, part-time teachers, administration, travel, and salaries.

Phase Three (FY1982-83)

As retrenchment continued, consequences to the district became more severe, although percentage reductions were no greater than before. Entire areas that the district considered central to its mission were eliminated, including retraining and employee development, library acquisition, and capital development.

Also severely affected were student services (such as counseling, services to minorities, and student placement), affirmative action, instructional programs, and institutional support services.

Phase Four (FY1983 to the Present)

The full impact of budget reductions probably will bring about a different configuration for SCCD. To date there have been no major changes to the district configuration, but it is likely that such will occur as a result of current analysis being undertaken by several districtwide task forces, which are developing a revised mission and goals statement and reviewing both organizational structure and budget mechanisms of the district. These efforts and others scheduled to follow are expected to result in systems that will help deal with future changes, both positive and negative.

Overall structure of the district remains basically the same, but there have been several specific alterations in organization effected since 1979-80. In the late seventies, for example, the district had approximately 100 administrators, whereas there were less than 70 in 1983-84. These reductions caused the aggregation of some instructional departments into larger divisions under control of one rather than two administrators. In addition, certain services have been eliminated and duties associated with eliminated positions have been transferred to others in the organization. These changes are scheduled for review by the chancellor.

Impact of Retrenchment

To comply with the governor's mandated reductions of 10% in September 1981, each of SCCD's campuses, as well as the district office, prepared reduction plans. Every effort was made to keep all constituencies informed and solicit their suggestions to the extent possible within the short two-week period allowed for submission of plans to comply with the order. At the district level, the chancellor's cabinet, composed of district officers and campus presidents, met with the president and vice-presidents of the Seattle Community College Federation of Teachers (SCCFT) to review budget implications of reductions. The district also met with SCCD officers from the Washington Federation of State Employees (WFSE) to obtain their suggestions.

The projected impact of the 10.1% cut was a 6% reduction in the 1981–82 base budget for salaries and a 13% reduction in the corresponding base budget for operations. Projected reductions for FY1982–83 total base budget were 11%, which meant a 9% reduction in the salary component and a 16% reduction in operating funds.

Specific areas affected by the 10.1% cut in 1981 included:

- Reduction of at least 90–100 equivalent positions, primarily by eliminating part-time positions, by voluntarily reducing working hours, and by not filling vacant positions.

- Reduction in library services, hours, and acquisitions.

- Severe reduction in maintenance and custodial services.

- Cutbacks in operation of facilities on weekends and evenings.

As mentioned earlier, these reductions were partially mitigated by a 5% restoration that occurred three months later in December 1981. Of the restored amount, 74% went to instruction, 13% to plant operations and maintenance, 6% to institutional support, 6% to student services, and 1% to libraries.

Staff Reductions

Restoration meant fewer reductions in staff than first anticipated. Total staff reductions for SCCD as a whole for FY1981–82 were 42.63 positions, with largest reductions—17.96 positions—being absorbed by the program area of instruction. Student services was reduced by 9.16 positions and plant operations and maintenance by 8.71 positions. Those affected included exempt administrative staff, full-time and part-time faculty, classified staff, and students on the work-study program.

Changes in Enrollment and Funding Sources

Because of budget cuts during the previous biennium (1979–81), the total number of FTE students served by SCCD in 1981–82 was 2,696 less than the corresponding number served during 1980–81 (12,616 vs. 15,312). There was a further drop of 112 total FTEs for 1982–83.

The 1981 reductions produced some changes in distribution of student FTEs by funding source. For academic year 1980–81, 94% were state-supported; 4%, locally supported; and 2%, by grants and contracts. During the following year, 88% were state-supported; 2.5%, locally supported; and 9.6%, by grants and contracts. These figures indicate that the biggest shift occurred in students supported by federal grants and contracts, which increased by 7.5 percentage points from 1980–81 to 1981–82. Conversely, the number of state-supported FTEs declined by six percentage points over the same period.

SCCD faced additional reductions in 1982–83. First, two separate reductions of 2% each were imposed—$544,000 by the legislature and $541,000 by the governor. Second, there was another shortfall of $20 million in state revenues, which translated into a cut of $350,000 for SCCD. Total reductions, therefore, amounted to approximately $1,354,000.

Use of Merit Pool Funds

To deal with these new budget cuts, at least two new courses of action were considered, both concerning use of funds appropriated by the 1981 legislature for faculty "merit increases." One alternative was for the governor to use these funds (roughly $6.8 million statewide) to offset a portion of the $20 million shortfall. Another was for SCCD to use its share of "merit pool" funds to offset the $1.3 million reduction.

According to then existing policy, merit pool funds could not be used to pay costs other than merit increases. Amounts dedicated for merit increases could, however, be decreased to the same degree that the legislature had reduced general appropriations for the community college system. Because the governor had ordered an additional $3.9 million of 1982–83 appropriated funds to be placed in reserves and because the state legislature reduced total community college funds by an additional $7.4 million (in addition to which there was the share from the $20 million shortfall), the policy of the State Board for Community College Education was changed regarding the use of merit funds: individual campuses were now given the option to use such funds as a partial offset to appropriation reductions and gubernatorial fund reservations. Responding to this option, SCCD decided to allocate its merit pool funds (2.1% of the budget) for salary-increase purposes. This decision was prompted by the minimal salary increases of the previous two years and the future outlook for such increases, which was bleak.

Lagged Payroll and Leave Without Pay

The governor instituted additional measures to cope with the $20-million shortfall. A ten-day lagged payroll system was implemented, yielding some $4 million in interest earnings and cost savings for the state as a whole, which in turn lessened the original reduction for SCCD from $350,000 to $288,000. The governor also established a voluntary leave-without-pay program, with an average two days' leave without pay for each state employee, including exempt personnel, to yield approximately $6.4 million in savings, assuming total participation.

Revenue collections for the 1981–83 biennium were well below forecasts made after the last two reductions of 2% each. State general fund revenues for the 1981–83 biennium were estimated at $9.7 billion. Actual revenues for the period were $8.5 billion, $1.2 billion or $12% below forecasts.

Early in FY1982–83 the district's appropriation was cut by an additional 5%. Because this reduction was anticipated, both campuses and district office built contingencies into their 1982–83 beginning budgets. In addition, all ending budget balances from 1981–82 (roughly $100,000), which usually are retained for the following year, were used to partially fund the cut. Furthermore, approximately $350,000 in year-end encumbrances for goods ordered but not received was used to fund part of the deficit. This meant that goods that should have been paid from 1981–82 funds carried forward (in accordance with historical practice) were charged to the already reduced 1982–83 budgets: a not-so-sophisticated budget cut.

For biennium 1983–85, forecasts of statewide revenues and expenditures indicated that revenues would fall $1.5–1.7 billion short of program needs. Clearly, additional reductions of such magnitude would necessarily entail significant changes in or even elimination of programs and services, or "radical modifications to the structure and process through which the campuses and the district office provide educational services to the community." To help cope with this major budget crisis, an ad hoc budget planning task force was formed primarily to review various alternatives for implementing budget cuts, with emphasis on issues that had districtwide implications. Suggestions offered by this committee include consideration of a four-day week, closure during Christmas – New Year's break, reduced number of weekly work hours (such as 36 or 38 paid hours versus 40), and reduced contract lengths for both faculty and administrators.

Funding Outlook for 1983–85

In order to respond to threatened erosion of the state community college system, the Washington state legislature enacted during the close of the 1982–83 legislative session some changes from which community colleges are likely to benefit. The budget adopted for the 1983–85 biennium incorporated increases in support for community colleges. Although increases were modest, they nevertheless came after nearly two years of budget cuts, staff and program reductions, and enrollment declines.

The total state general fund appropriation for the community college system for 1983–85 is $436.6 million. This is $711,000 less than the level recommended by the governor, but it actually provides a higher support level because the governor expected the system to serve 86,000 FTEs in 1984–85, or 3,000 more second-year FTEs than were anticipated in the budget adopted by the legislature.

Excluding funds earmarked for salary and benefit increases, the community college budget consists of five major pieces:

- $232.5 million appropriated for instruction.

- $9.7 million appropriated for replacement and repair of instructional equipment.

- $3.3 million appropriated for small school adjustment.

- $75 million appropriated for instructional support resources, which include libraries and student services.

- $114 million appropriated for general purposes, which include plant maintenance, institutional support (administration), and state board operations.

Certain measures were taken in an effort to preserve educational quality. For example, the $232 million appropriated for instruction is conditional on the following:

> Average basic direct instructional resource per comparable cost student shall not be less than $1,400 per academic year averaged for the biennium. Faculty full-time equivalent entitlements for direct instructional purposes shall not be less than 3,657 per year and shall not fall below the overall student-to-faculty ratio as calculated in the governor's budget request.

This proviso represents the heart of the new funding method which stresses quality through maintenance of student/faculty ratios rather than growth as measured in FTEs. In 1983, the state legislature defined specific allowable limits, both over and under the legislatively set FTE student-support levels. Variances in excess of either of these limits are now subject to significant reductions in next year's appropriation. This has eliminated or at least severely reduced the tendency to "do whatever is necessary" to accommodate student demand, including such actions as dilution of the student-faculty ratio, reducing percentage of full-time faculty, and reducing levels of support services. Although this process maintains a higher-quality level of instruction, it leaves the district unable to serve many persons seeking a community college education.

Another proviso provides a limited degree of flexibility by stipulating that money may be transferred from instructional support resources to basic instruction, but not vice versa. This new legislation also recognizes that community colleges may be tied even more closely to serving growth industries within local areas and throughout the state. In this regard, the legislative provision notes that:

> The state board shall review and modify its allocation methods for enrollments to recognize any recent change in student demand and needs. In determining demand and needs, the state board shall consider the needs of new industries, with special reference to the semi-conductor industry, and any other state economic growth that community college education can enhance in rural as well as metropolitan areas.

Another bill enacted during the 1982–83 legislative session established a Youth Conservation Corps and directed participating state agencies to develop agreements with community colleges to provide special education in basic skills. Classes would be conducted outside corps members' regularly scheduled working hours.

Summary

Seattle Community College District (SCCD) was established to serve diverse needs of the local community. The district's two major concerns of providing access to students and providing services to the local community, however, have been adversely affected to a great degree by state funding cutbacks that were implemented from 1979 to 1982; the cuts substantially reduced course offerings and class sections and limited the access of a significant number of students who previously were served by the district. Even for existing students, services were cut; for example, counseling was centralized and correspondingly reduced in the process.

Retrenchment was particularly traumatic for SCCD because neither the occurrence nor the magnitude of reductions was fully anticipated.

Even when approximate amounts of state appropriation cutbacks were known, frequent changes in implementation decisions at the state level and occasionally inadequate communication between the state govern' ment and various institutions further compounded SCCD's difficulties. Despite this, SCCD, aided in part by new legislation, is trying to refor' mulate its mission so that its long-term stability as an institution and that of the entire community college system is preserved.

References

Managing Contraction (An Institution Experiences Contraction) by John Casey, 1982.

The University of Idaho

Long-range planning has begun, involving all aspects of the campus, and is expected to create renewed enthusiasm for a brighter future.

Between 1979 and 1983, major changes occurred in Idaho. Concurrently, the citizens voted to limit property taxes and the national recession hit the state's largest industries; these factors seriously affected state economy and revenues. In addition, a destructive prison riot necessitated major construction and out-of-state boarding of prisoners, and unanticipated cleanup expenses resulted from the spilling of volcanic ash over much of northern Idaho by the eruption of Mount St. Helen's. These events contributed to a severe drain on state general funds. A series of budget reductions followed, and the University of Idaho found itself facing retrenchment and reallocation on a scale unprecedented in its nearly 100-year history.

Institutional Profile

Founded in 1889, a year before Idaho became a state, the University of Idaho is the state's flagship, land-grant institution. It has been designated by the board of regents as Idaho's primary graduate education and research institution. The fall 1982 headcount enrollment was 9,185 (8,077 FTEs), with 56% in the lower division, 33% in the upper division, and 11% at graduate and professional levels. The university offers 152 academic programs within the colleges of agriculture; art and architecture; business and economics; engineering; education; forestry, wildlife, and range science; law; mines and earth resources; and letters and science.

The University of Idaho is governed by a board of regents which also serves concurrently as trustees of the other two public universities—Idaho State University at Pocatello and Boise State University at Boise—and as trustees of Lewis-Clark State College, a small four-year institution in Lewiston. The same group also comprises the state board of education, which is responsible for kindergarten through high school public education. The board, supported by a small staff in Boise, is headed by an executive director and governs the four postsecondary institutions through loosely defined role and mission statements. Until 1983, the board had not attempted to make much distinction between specified roles and missions for the four institutions.

Funding for the institutions comes from allocations made by the board from a lump-sum appropriation by the state legislature for "colleges and universities." Historically, the board has divided the lump-sum appropriation among the institutions in essentially the same percentage shares as each previous year's allocation. In the last two years, the board has attempted to refine allocation to make it more sensitive to enrollment changes and shifts, as well as more reflective of role and mission assignments.

In addition to this "general education" budget support, the University of Idaho receives direct, line-item appropriations from the state legislature for the Agricultural Research and Extension Service program, and separate appropriations for the Washington-Oregon-Idaho (WOI) regional program in veterinary medicine, the Washington-Alaska-Montana-Idaho (WAMI) regional medical education program, and the Forest Utilization Research program. These separate appropriations are significant because neither the board nor the university is allowed to move funds among or between them; nor is the university allowed to move funds between these appropriations and its general education allocation. Thus, when the legislature mandates a specific salary increase but fails to fund its added cost (as in FY1980), the separately appropriated program areas cannot be helped by the board's using some land-grant endowment income reserve and/or increase in student fees to partially offset the salary increase cost burden.

Chronology

Idaho's budgetary difficulties began in November 1978, when voters approved a 1% property tax limit initiative mandating the legislature to enact limits to property taxes not to exceed 1% of the market value of assessed property and to limit future adjustments for inflation to not exceed 5% in any one year. This initiative resulted in reducing local support for public schools (as well as city and county governments) significantly. In addition, Idaho was obligated to increase its support for public schools to offset loss of local property taxes. The state legislature elected to implement the mandate by shifting state revenues rather than increasing them. The obvious result was that the share of state revenues supporting public elementary and high schools rose and the share going to higher education (as well as some other state services supported by state tax revenues) dropped dramatically.

Figure 1 shows what happened during the period of this study. It compares the annual change in support for public schools with the overall change in state revenues and the change in state general account support for colleges and universities.

In addition to the voter-approved property tax limitation, the state encountered other circumstances that adversely affected its economy and ability to adequately support services. A major prison uprising destroyed a significant portion of the state's large prison facility, requiring Idaho to send prisoners to neighboring states for confinement. This cost and that of repairing the damaged facility, plus the legislature's recognition that more state support for its Department of Corrections was needed on a continuing basis, placed unexpected burdens on an

Figure 1

Annual Percent Change
State General Account

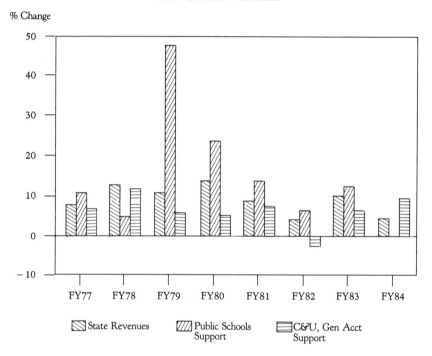

% Change

already overburdened state treasury. The eruption of Mount St. Helen's, which spread volcanic ash over large sections of northern Idaho, affected state economic health in two ways: cleanup costs were sizeable but, more significantly, tourism in northern Idaho was nearly eliminated for the remainder of the year.

Just as the state was adjusting to these problems, it was struck by the full weight of the national recession. Agriculture, forestry, mining, and tourism are the principal contributors to the state's economy. Unlike previous recessions that had little impact on Idaho, the recession of the late 70s and early 80s significantly affected the state. Major sectors of the forest and mining industries closed down and unemployment reached all-time highs.

These developments, as well as adjustments for inflation during this period, meant the state had to struggle to support its agencies and institutions. Appropriations fell short of inflationary growth in costs of doing business. State revenues during fiscal years 1979–82 failed to reach even conservative projections of the legislature, forcing the governor to hold back appropriated funds to keep the budget in balance (required by the state constitution). Not until FY1983 did the legislature act midyear to increase state revenues through a temporary sales tax in order to partially make up for expected shortfalls in state income. Until then the brunt of Idaho's financial problems was borne by state agencies and institutions. A state law required any shortfall in appropriated funds for public schools to be made up by a special local property tax, but the governor was reluctant to shift the state's revenue problem back to local property taxpayers by withholding funds appropriated for public schools. Thus, remaining state-supported services, of which higher education was largest, carried the burden of the state's financial stress.

Table I summarizes the specific events in the period FY1979 through FY1983 that affected the University of Idaho.

Table I

Chronology

Date	Action
FY 1979	*November*—Idaho voters approve the 1% tax initiative.
	September through April—University staff prepare at least eight different budget scenarios for internal use and for the board, the governor's staff, and/or the legislature budget office staff.
	March—Legislature appropriates for FY1980 an increase of 2.5% for higher education, but mandates a 7% salary increase.
	April—Board adopts a new reduction-in-force policy to deal with employee layoffs under conditions of financial exigency.
	May—Board declares a state of financial exigency for the separately appropriated Agriculture Research and Extension Service, and raises student fees for partial support of college and university general education budgets.
FY1980	*July*—University must reduce its budget by $3.2 million.
	March—Legislature appropriates for FY1981 a 9.2% increase for higher education.
FY1981	*August*—Governor orders a 3.0% holdback in state general account funds.

October—Governor orders an additional .85% holdback.

Board raises student fees temporarily for second semester. University reduces its operating budget by $1.4 million.

March—Legislature appropriates for FY 1982 a 4.4% increase for higher education.

April—Board declares a state of financial exigency for FY 1982.

FY 1982   *March*—Legislature appropriates for FY 1983 a 7.6% increase for higher education.

May—Governor orders a 3.7% holdback in state general account, and a 32-hour work week for those state employees who are paid from state general account, as partial solution to holdback problem. The reduced workweek order affects about one-third of university faculty and staff.

June—State auditor delays paying some payroll and other invoice obligations until after the start of the next fiscal year, in order to maintain the state treasury's positive fund balance.

FY 1983   *July*—Governor orders a 9% holdback of state general account funds. The university is required to reduce budgets by $2.8 million. The board declares a state of financial exigency, and approves student fee increases for new academic year. Institutional plans for budget reductions, including reductions-in-force, are approved by board.

October—Governor orders an additional 1.5% holdback, costing the university another $638,900.

March—Legislature enacts a temporary 1.5% sales tax increase, to end June 30, 1984. It appropriates a 4.2% increase for FY 1984 for higher education operating budgets.

June—Governor allocates an additional $3 million for higher education to be added to operating budgets. The board divides funds among institutions, but the State Board of Examiners approves only $2 million of governor's allocation. Higher education institutions start the FY 1984 operating year with a $1 million deficit in appropriated funds. The board and governor submit a supplemental appropriation request to the legislature for the $1 million makeup.

Impact of Financial Stress

The full impact of the changing financial support described above may not be totally realized for several years. However, some effects are evident today. In the period between FY1979 and FY1984, the university had to eliminate 264 positions, over 15% of total faculty and staff. Although the university tried to anticipate budget reductions and, therefore, freeze positions that became vacant or transfer personnel from affected positions to other institutional employment, 54 people received termination or layoff notices. The breakdown of affected positions by category is:

    25 Tenured faculty
    83 Nontenured faculty
    21 Nonfaculty professional staff
   135 Classified (secretarial, clerical, technical)

The share of state general account appropriated to higher education dropped from 20.8% in FY1978 to below 15% in FY1983. Enrollment during that period increased 9.4% for all campuses and 10.2% for the University of Idaho. Thus, state general account support per FTE student declined over 26% in the five-year period. Student fees, on the other hand, increased 86% in the same period. However, because most of the student fee historically has been dedicated to such non-appropriated functions as athletics and auxiliary enterprises, the real increase in student contribution to the institution's noninstructional general education operations increased nearly 600% in the last five years. Nonresident tuition increased about 70%. Faculty/staff turnover rose from a typical annual average of about 3% to over 12% in FY1983.

Responses to Financial Stress

In dealing with financial stress, the University of Idaho used a variety of strategies and responses that had both internal and external involvements, and were strongly influenced by the timing of particular budget crises. For example, midyear holdbacks generally necessitated short-term responses that would not affect contractual obligations with employees or disrupt academic programs. In contrast, responses to funding shortfalls affecting the entire fiscal year generally encompassed more permanent reductions in operations, including programs and personnel reductions.

In the sections below, specific actions of the university are described and strategic responses to fiscal stress are examined.

Short-Term Responses

During the period of financial stress, the university often had to respond to midyear budget reductions created by state general account holdbacks ordered by the governor. Since most employees are on either annual or indefinite appointment contracts and the students were already enrolled in their courses by midyear, university administrators turned to short-term solutions, including use of one-time funds to replace lost state general account funds, or elimination or deferral of expenditures where no contractual obligations existed. These temporary responses included:

Freezing vacant positions and using "salary savings" as a one-time funds source.

University level operating contingency reserves committed as another source to offset general account losses.

Funds budgeted initially for capital equipment purchases, facility maintenance and improvement projects, and other nonpersonnel operating expenses such as travel reduced to help cover general account reductions. Some expenditures deferred and others eliminated.

Long-Term Responses

The university adopted various long-term responses at both state/board and campus levels.

State/Board Level. The president gained maximum flexibility in allocating funds by asking the legislature to change from its line-item appropriation by number of FTE positions and by expenditure class (that is, personnel services, operating expense, and capital outlay) to a lump-sum, single-line appropriation to the board for the four institutions. The board, in turn, allocated to each institution a lump-sum amount. The desire of industry representatives to maintain visibility of legislative appropriations for special program areas (Agricultural Research and Extension Service and WOI Veterinary Medicine Program) kept each of these areas separate from the university's general education programs funding.

University administrators worked with the board and its staff to develop a procedure for distributing the lump-sum appropriation to campuses that was more equitable than the historic process of using the previous year's percentages. Cost analyses using Information Exchange

Procedures (IEP), developed by the National Center for Higher Education Management Systems (NCHEMS), were initiated by the board in an attempt to define equity. The university received an additional $634,000 through "equity adjustments" in FY1981 through FY1983.

The university increased its advancement efforts with major businesses and industries in the northwest by explaining the state funding plight and seeking financial and political support. Private giving to the University Foundation has grown nearly 20% in each of the last five years.

Campus Level. At the campus level, the university adopted several approaches to meet reductions in state support. Administrators focused on selective program or service reductions or complete elimination as opposed to across-the-board budget reductions. Programs that received reduced state support included training for office administrators, music, biological science, geology field camp, continuing education administration, and student services. Programs and services that were eliminated included the Center for Native American Studies, Upward Bound, Afro-American Studies, museology, summer theatre, and several foreign language programs.

Retirements and terminations released funds for reallocation, or permitted elimination of positions in selected program or service areas. Early retirement incentives were offered on a selective basis, with consideration given to reducing investment in specific program or service areas.

Several consolidations of administrative units in both academic and nonacademic areas were implemented. Emphasis was placed on eliminating duplication of function or service (such as consolidation of teaching of statistics by numerous departments in several colleges into one combined Department of Mathematics and Applied Statistics), and on reducing strata of administration levels (for example, elimination of director of institutional services' position and assignment of staff to report to the president or to other department heads within the administrative services area, or directly to the financial vice president).

(a) Academic Area Responses

The emphasis was on program reduction or elimination, rather than on personnel layoff. Criteria used to determine programs for reduction or elimination included (1) centrality to institution's mission, (2) service to other programs in the university, (3) program uniqueness in state and region, (4) enrollment demand, (5) overall quality and productivity, (6) potential organizational consolidation, (7) program costs—both absolute and relative, (8) accreditation status, if applicable, and (9) importance to maintenance of a resident student community.

Enrollment limitations were imposed on some program areas where resource allocations could not keep up with increasing student demand. However, the board was reluctant to change Idaho's historic open admissions policy and impose general enrollment limitations for any institution.

Faculty development programs were organized whereby faculty in low enrollment program areas could retrain in other program areas in which student demand was increasing. Faculty interest in computer science was given high priority.

(b) Nonacademic Area Responses

Early in budget reduction planning, the president mandated a two-dollar reduction in nonacademic areas (such as institutional management, physical plant, and student services) for each dollar reduction in academic program areas. In addition to organizational consolidations and elimination of some midlevel administrative positions, the university completed a thorough review of its major administrative procedures and business practices. These reviews were designated as "paperflow workshops" and they resulted in some policy changes, relaxation or elimination of certain internal controls, and modification of many internal procedures to streamline business practices on campus.

In some service areas, such as campus recreation programs and issuance of student identification, user fees either were increased or newly established to reduce appropriated funds support for the activity.

Major emphasis was placed on improving communications between academic and financial administrative offices to avoid decisions that would create permanent funding obligations without necessary financial resources to support future commitments.

Strategic Responses

In addition to specific short-term and long-term actions described above, the university used various general strategic responses to deal with problems of financial stress. These included:

- Maximum use of funds allocation flexibility.

- Establishing budget reduction guidelines: nonacademic versus academic budget cuts.

- Program versus performance evaluations.

- Constituency participation.

Maximum Use of Funds Allocation Flexibility

Because of actions by the state legislature and the board of regents, the University of Idaho was able to take full advantage of flexibility in funds allocation, which has been a key contributor to helping the university "weather the storm." The benefit of flexibility manifested itself in several ways. First, the university did not have to be concerned about numbers of employee FTEs appropriated or about specific appropriations for such items as personnel services, travel, or equipment; thus, it could more easily address needs to reallocate funds internally. With the lifting of certain state-imposed restrictions, the administration could more freely evaluate alternatives that involved possible shifts in budget from one expenditure category to another.

Flexibility was passed on to colleges and nonacademic units on campus. While control over "permanent" personnel positions was retained at administration levels, all support budget allocations (such as funds for hourly employee wages, travel, office, instructional expenses, and equipment) were distributed in lump sums. Colleges and departments had broad flexibility in assigning their allocation to various budgeted expenses categories. The only major requirement was that they submit annual budget plans and even those could be modified during the year by moving funds from one budget category to another without university administration review and approval.

As university administrators used flexibility in allocating budget reductions where needed, individual colleges and departments also were encouraged to do the same and not just make across-the-board cuts. They were asked to look at their total budgets, including personnel, in preparing recommendations. This helped them focus on specific reductions rather than be overly concerned with the appropriateness of shifting funds between expenditure categories.

A significant use of flexibility involved taking advantage of the university's constitutional status in terms of how it manages that portion of appropriated funds derived from local revenue dollars. A part of the legislative appropriation includes income from student fees, land-grant endowments, and some sales and services. Such income is managed locally by the University of Idaho rather than being deposited in the state treasury, as is the case for the other three institutions controlled by the board of regents. Previously, the university indicated to its colleges and departments that any funds not expended by the end of a fiscal year would revert to the state treasury. While this is true for the state tax revenue portion of the total university appropriation, the reversion does not apply to local funds.

During the period of financial stress, the administration extended a carry-forward capability to all campus colleges and departments. By careful assignment of sources of funds to be used for payroll and other expenses, the university could control those sources that remained unobligated at the end of the fiscal year, and yet be certain that no state tax revenues reverted. Colleges and departments were encouraged to be mainly concerned with conserving resources and getting the most out of their allocation, since particular sources of appropriated funds were not apparent. The result was a significant reduction in year-end purchases and the carrying forward of small balances to compensate partially for support budget reductions. In some instances, carry-forward balances were combined with the previous year's reserves and then used for such purposes as acquisition of equipment or faculty conference expenses that otherwise could not have been covered by any single year's allocation. To encourage good management of allocated support budget funds, the administration at no time considered these modest carry-forward reserve balances a source of funds to offset loss of general account money.

Establishing Budget Reduction Guidelines: Nonacademic versus Academic Budget Cuts

It was stated that early in budget reduction planning, the university president mandated a $2 reduction in nonacademic departmental budgets for each $1 reduction in academic areas. This initial strategy has since been adopted as the basis for internal allocation of any newly appropriated funds. As a result, the university's expenditure pattern shows approximately 60% total appropriated funds being directly expended for teaching, research, and public service, a ratio that is in sharp contrast to the 45% that is typically spent by other, similar institutions for these functions.

The benefits of using these resource reallocation criteria have been at least twofold. First, by setting criteria early in the period of financial stress, the university avoided the danger of adopting easily implemented, short-term solutions, such as eliminating a few more support staff positions or decreasing frequency of maintenance activities. The criteria thus helped to focus decision making.

Second, the criteria forced thorough evaluation of ways the university conducted its business, such as the paperflow process, and of how it was organized to deliver services both internally and to outside constituencies. Such introspection has created a general sense of willingness to try new approaches where warranted and to make improvements.

Increasing capabilities and productivity of existing staff is emphasized rather than adding more staff as workload increases. For example, the university made significant investments in electronic communication, data processing, and word processing systems that integrate these func' tions into single work stations. Paperless transactions were im' plemented, thereby cutting processing time from weeks and days to minutes (the university received a NACUBO—U.S. Steel Foundation Cost Reduction Incentive Award in 1982 for its electronic, budget' adjustment process).

There is enthusiasm on campus about these achievements, but the question remains regarding the most appropriate ratio between univer' sity expenditures for teaching, research, and public service on the one hand and for support services to these primary mission activities on the other. The administration believes that the current expenditure "effi' ciency ratio" of 60% academic to 40% nonacademic is close to optimal, but there is some uneasiness about certain low nonacademic resource commitments, particularly in student services and facility maintenance. On the whole, however, the administration views the institution as being more efficient and effective than it was in the past.

Program versus Performance Evaluations

The extent of financial crisis made personnel reductions unavoidable. From the first budget reduction throughout the entire financial stress period, the university used program evaluations rather than performance evaluations to reduce personnel positions. In a few instances, such as in the Agricultural Research and Extension Service, a small program effort might be supported by a single personnel position. However, even in these cases, criteria for program review and elimination were broader than those of a performance review of a specific staff member.

Personnel reduction through program evaluations was criticized, primarily by off'campus constituencies. The common complaint was that budget cuts should be used "to weed out the deadwood," but there was little agreement on who the "deadwood" were. The university main' tained that it would be bad management to eliminate a personnel posi' tion in an important program area because of a vacancy or poor per' formance of the incumbent. It was felt that making personnel decisions on such a basis was a short'term move that could lower the quality of many good programs.

In evaluating programs, the university assumed that decisions on pro' gram reductions or eliminations would be permanent, and that funds to rebuild affected programs would not be available in the immediate future. Furthermore, administrators avoided controversial questions about competency reviews that could lead to lawsuits.

Constituency Participation

Campus constituencies participated in several ways in developing plans for budget reductions. During FY1979 efforts to develop several budget-cutting scenarios, the president formed a special budget planning committee composed of the academic and financial vice presidents, executive assistant to the president and coordinator of student services, two deans, chairman of the faculty council, three members of the faculty council's budget liaison committee, and the student body president. The committee's detailed work served as a basis for many decisions on budget reductions that were necessitated by later crises.

The dean's council, when attended by the faculty council chairperson and members of that council's budget committee, helped the administration formulate budget plans on a continuing basis in response to other mandated permanent reductions of programs or services. Nonacademic department heads and the staff affairs council, representing nonfaculty professional and classified staff, were also consulted in decision making.

Other Factors Affecting Strategic Responses

The university's strategic responses to financial stress were aided by the following positive factors: (1) great flexibility in allocation and expenditure of funds; (2) decision-making emphasis regarding proportional budget cuts in academic versus nonacademic areas; and (3) focus on program rather than performance evaluations to implement both faculty and staff reductions.

However, administrators also encountered constraints and hindrances, which included:

- Need for more definite board guidelines on setting program priorities.

- Political pressure.

- Layoff or transfer of tenured faculty.

- Obligation to students enrolled in discontinued progams.

- Need for more concrete long-range plans.

Need for Clear Board Guidelines

One difficulty encountered by the university in making decisions on program reductions or eliminations was lack of board involvement and absence of clear board guidelines on setting program priorities. In the absence of such guidelines, administrators generally assumed that program eliminations at the university could lead to establishing these programs at other institutions. Such a development could in turn lead to loss of students and corresponding funds. It was rarely assumed that the size of the appropriations pie itself would shrink.

The board partially addressed this problem in the last year. Two exercises in 1983 organized by board staff attempted to define more specifically the roles and missions of each institution. However, these redefinitions may be more useful for future planning purposes than for purposes of program elimination.

Political Pressure

Political pressure sometimes affected reduction or elimination of certain university program efforts, particularly in agriculture, which involved statewide activity. For example, area industry groups and local politicians opposed the closing of an experimental station. The need for budget cuts was clear, but there was disagreement on where cuts should be made.

Throughout the five-year stress period, the university continued to develop and use defensible criteria for program eliminations, even though the criteria were not accepted to the same degree by all groups.

Layoff or Transfer of Tenured Faculty

In the Spring of 1979, the board adopted a new "reduction-in-force" policy to deal with personnel layoff, including tenured faculty, under a state of financial exigency. A key element of that policy was that a layoff could be implemented after a 30-day notice, following a formal declaration of a state of financial exigency by the board. This very short time frame continues to be a major concern.

The university attempted to cushion the impact of layoffs by making a major effort to transfer the person in the affected position to an unaffected position. In most cases when people received layoff notices, transfers were implemented before a break in pay occurred. In a few cases within the classified staff category, layoff rosters were created and people on these rosters were given first priority for new vacancies, when qualified. Finally, in a few situations involving layoff of tenured faculty, the university was able to retain the faculty member through the academic year by using one-time funding sources. Only in one case was the university unable to place a tenured faculty member in another acceptable position.

Students Enrolled in Discontinued Programs

One retrenchment issue relates to the legal or moral obligation of an institution to students enrolled in a program that is identified for elimination prior to students' completion of their coursework. At the University of Idaho, most academic program cuts were in areas with very small enrollment. In those few cases where students were affected, special arrangements were made to accommodate their needs, including the use of Washington State University, only eight miles away.

Need for Long-Range Planning

Lack of a comprehensive, long-range plan for the university presented difficulties during the budget cutback period. When the institution first experienced financial stress in FY1978 and FY1979, the relatively new administration had to deal with one budget crisis after another, guided essentially by a broadly defined role and mission statement rather than by a specific long-range plan. Need for long-range planning was recognized, but not until FY1984 was there an opportunity to seriously work toward developing such a plan. However, this activity was recently begun, with the first board review scheduled for spring of 1984.

Future Outlook

Follow-up discussions with staff at the University of Idaho indicate considerable optimism about the future. The recession appears to have "bottomed out." State revenues have stabilized and the state's general economy is improving. Business and industry leaders are taking a more active role in promoting funding needs of higher education to political leadership in the state. Private giving, which has been actively solicited by the university, continues to increase significantly and emphasis will be placed on such giving in connection with celebrating the university's 100th birthday in 1989. Long-range planning, which involves all aspects of the campus, is expected to create renewed enthusiasm and concentrate on a brighter future.

References

FY1979–80 Budget Plan (describes retrenchment in its initial phases).

"The Idaho Experience," by David L. McKinney. *Responses to Fiscal Stress in Higher Education,* Robert A. Wilson, Ed., Tucson, AZ: Center for the Study of Higher Education, University of Arizona, June 1982.

Overview of Financial Condition, Operating Budgets FY1979–FY1984 (prepared by the University of Idaho's Budget Office; February 1983).

State Board of Education Multi-Year Financial Study (November 1982).

Michigan State University

Maintaining academic excellence in the midst of changing financial conditions demands constant attention to the university's mission and goals, and requires a continuous process of universitywide strategic planning.

The 1983 quotation from Michigan State University, used to open this chapter, indicates concern with universitywide planning. But is unlikely that Michigan State University (MSU) or any other institution of higher education would have recognized the importance of linkages among financial resources, academic quality, and program review during the expansionist 1960s. The operating principles during that period seemed to be that "more is better" and that financial resources were at hand to produce more. Two factors shaped MSU's current thinking on academic planning: (1) wisdom of hindsight and (2) rigors of planning during the financial crisis.

Institutional Profile

Michigan State University, established in 1855, has been a land-grant institution since 1863 and has developed into a major research institution, becoming a member of the Association of American Universities in 1964. In the process, the university greatly expanded the scope and depth of its program offerings through additional departments, colleges, and professional schools. For example, it instituted two new medical colleges—allopathic in 1964 and osteopathic in 1969.

Enrollments also grew tremendously, nearly doubling between 1960 and 1983. In 1960, enrollment was 23,700. By 1966, it had grown to 41,500, and in fall 1980, enrollment was at 47,300.

By 1980, however, state support for higher education had declined. In 1980–81, higher education, including community colleges, received 16.9% of the 1980–81 state general fund budget, down from 20.7% in 1966–67. Four-year institutions received 14.2% of the 1980–81 state general fund budget, down from 19.1% in 1966–67. Michigan State University received 19.4% of the 1980–81 state general fund budget appropriation for four-year institutions, down from 22.4% in 1966–67.

Even by national standards, the state's support for higher education declined. Per capita state-funded appropriations to higher education in Michigan fell from a rank of seventh nationally in 1966–67 to twenty-ninth in 1980–81. State-funded appropriations per $1000 of personal income to higher education fell from a rank of nineteenth in 1966–67 to thirty-eighth in 1980–81.

Partly to offset declining state support, tuition revenues were increased. Tuition at Michigan's public four-year colleges and universities is among the highest nationally of public institutions. In fall 1980, resident undergraduate tuition at MSU ranked eighth highest in the membership survey of the National Association of State Universities and Land-Grant Colleges.

By 1980, it was clear that the expansion of previous years could not continue, given declining state support. A fiscal crisis, manifested in drastic reductions in state support during Fiscal Year 1980–81, underscored the point further and led to long-range planning for realloca- tion and retrenchment. This case history describes how MSU dealt with immediate financial problems and planned for contraction.

Chronology

Financial crisis came first. As with other public institutions, MSU's budgetary problems were tied to the state economy. Michigan's economy in 1980 was on a precipitous downward spiral, with little pro- bability of a rapid, major turnaround. Unemployment was soaring and tax revenues were falling, requiring further state outlays. The state government had to meet a constitutional requirement for a balanced budget. Under these conditions, state agencies could expect executive orders for reductions and return of nonexpended fund balances.

The university also had a more immediate concern in 1980: five months into its fiscal year, it still did not have an appropriation from the state, and it did not reliably know how much support it could expect.

MSU had adopted a budget in September 1980, based on a 2.5% increase approved by the Michigan house earlier that month. Earlier in May, the senate had approved an increase amounting to 4%. However, the legislature was at an impasse over a final appropriation and passed a continuing spending resolution for the first quarter of the state fiscal year at 24% of the previous year's appropriation. In November, the legislature approved an appropriation that was 6.1% below that of the previous year. Suddenly, MSU faced a budget shortfall of $10.1 million on a $204 million budget, and it took several one-time measures to deal with this immediate problem. In November 1980, the university also began a long-range planning process.

For 1981–82, MSU projected another budget shortfall of $29.2 million. Continuing commitments and essential expenditure increases were calculated to be $225 million, but revenues, without considering increased state support, were estimated only at $195.8 million.

In February 1981, the university's board of trustees reviewed this fiscal assessment and declared that MSU was in a "state of financial crisis." It directed the president to produce a plan to resolve the crisis by the next board meeting, which was a month away. The university thus intensified its long-range planning process, begun the previous November, and by March 22, 1981, it presented the board with a plan for massive retrenchment and reallocation of the university's resources.

It proposed a total reduction of $19.1 million, of which the board approved $17 million.

MSU is currently in the process of implementing its retrenchment and reallocation plan. Table I summarizes these events.

Table I

Chronology

Date	Action
September 1980	Three months into its fiscal year, MSU adopts budget (based on an appropriation approved by the house) 2.5% more than previous year.
November 1980	State legislature approves an appropriation 6.1% below previous year.
December 1980	MSU takes one-time measures to deal with immediate shortfall.
February 1981	MSU projects budget shortfall of $29.2 million for 1981–82.
	Board of trustees declares institution to be in a "state of financial crisis." It directs university to develop a plan.
February–March 1981	MSU completes plans for reductions across all units of university.
March–April 1981	MSU proposes reductions of $19.1 million to board. Board reduces this to $17 million.
April 1981–Present	Plans for retrenchment and reallocation implemented.
October 1981	Financial crisis resolution withdrawn.

Approaches to Retrenchment and Reallocation

Within four months, Michigan State University implemented a two-phase approach to retrenchment: (1) one-time, across-the-board reductions, and (2) long-term planning to curtail the institution's size and scope. The first efforts were one-time events, and their effect on the institution's overall character was minimal. The long-range planning process, however, is critical to MSU's future and is clearly at the crux of retrenchment and reallocation at the university.

First Reductions

The university took four measures in December 1980 to eliminate the $10.1 million shortfall caused by lack of funds originally budgeted for Fiscal Year 1980–81 but not received. First, a $20 registration fee surcharge was implemented for the winter and spring terms, yielding approximately $1.6 million. Second, all but "essential" personnel were laid off for two and one-half days, yielding savings of $1.2 million. The order included administrators, faculty, and academic staff, and days designated for lay-off were chosen to be as nondisruptive as possible; they included the afternoon of December 24 and the full days of December 29 and December 31. The provost noted that a selective lay-off to achieve the same ends would require that 130 people be laid off for six months (assuming an average salary of $18,000).

As a third measure, special projects were deferred, amounting to a savings of $2.3 million. And fourth, across-the-board reductions totaling $5 million were ordered.

Proposals and Processes

In submitting long-term proposals for retrenchment and reallocation to the board of trustees in March 1981, MSU recognized that its financial situation required defining its mission more narrowly and reducing its programs and personnel.

> The one option we do not have is to recommend minimal changes or no changes. . . . The decision problem we face is radically different. Our decision problem is: "Which programs should be sustained and which should be curtailed or eliminated?" Michigan State University cannot be all things to all people. In fact, the university is not funded at a level which will allow it to continue all its current programs. (Coordinated Proposals. . . . 1981, page 2)

This recognition did not come easily. It emerged from an intensive, universitywide process of decision making on reallocation and retrenchment, which continues to the present.

Retrenchment and reallocation processes at MSU have been guided by a fundamental consideration: all programs and activities must be examined in terms of centrality to the university's role and mission. To comply with the board's directive to resolve the institution's financial crisis, MSU launched a series of campus planning activities. The president named a select advisory committee for university planning and priorities, which was responsible for advising him and the provost about program continuation, curtailment, and elimination. The committee was composed of 11 senior faculty members appointed jointly by the president and steering committee of the academic council.

Several substantive planning documents were developed: (1) a mission statement, drawing on the university's historical role of service, but addressed to the establishment of guiding principles and priorities in a period of limited resources; (2) criteria for program continuation and curtailment or elimination; and (3) a statement on organization and operating principles.

Long-Term Planning

The 1980–82 planning process at Michigan State University included:

- Continuous consultation with board of trustees.

- Developing a forum for suggestions and proposals.

- Planning for each vice presidential area.

- Coordination of planning among vice presidents.

- Parallel college and major administrative unit meetings.

- Consultation with appropriate constituencies.

- Impact assessment.

- Recommendations to board of trustees.

Several parameters were used in this decision-making process. First, faculty salary increases had to be sustained; the university required sufficient funds to keep it competitive with peer institutions. Second, staff increases had to be maintained at levels provided in collective bargaining contracts; third, tuition rate increases had to be held in the general range of the projected inflation rate for the coming year (tuition rates in professional health areas were a special case); fourth, anticipated appropriations from the state would be somewhat below the level reflected in the appropriations bill currently before the legislature; and finally, it was assumed that there would be no further major change in the Michigan economy that would have a significant impact on either the 1980–81 or 1981–82 general fund budget of MSU.

Target budget reductions were set for each university unit so that the total budget would meet reduction requirements. To formulate its own plan for retrenchment and reallocation, each unit developed planning activities and guidelines on how to meet its target budget.

The College of Education provides an example of the way this process worked. For consistency in nomenclature, the provost's guidelines were adopted with regard to these definitions: (1) *Reduction in effort—*reducing number of programs offered by the college and for which it takes responsibility; and (2) *Reduction in force—*reducing number of unit personnel on the university payroll.

The colleges as a unit had to plan first for a reduction of effort, which would then result in a reduction in force. Reductions in effort had to be based on qualitative criteria; remaining programs, therefore, had to be of at least the same and preferably of better quality than the other pro-grams that existed prior to the concerted planning effort. In addition to program quality indicators, reductions were to be made selectively within the framework of college mission and resources. Thus, planning documents required faculty to define their program in the overall context of being part of a professional College of Education, a land-grant university, and a university that belonged to the Association of American Universities. Planning activities for the College of Education required information on enrollments at undergraduate and graduate levels and estimates of number of faculty and support staff associated with a program, along with their salaries. The level of funded and non-funded research and service projects was also taken into consideration.

Each unit in the college then compiled a unit summary that ranked programs with their organizational components. Included in the summary was an assessment of which programs would be reduced, assuming a 10% budget reduction over several years, and a ranking by order of money saved. Units also had to report savings in faculty and support staff that would result if lowest-priority programs were discon-tinued, and to specify faculty essential to the quality of remaining unit programs, as well as those who would be terminated.

From processes such as these, each college made decisions on those programs to retain, reduce, or augment.

Impact of Retrenchment

Substantial cutbacks resulted from the university's planning process, enabling it to be better prepared for subsequent state reductions and any future financial difficulties.

Institutional Support Services

Total reductions in institutional support amounted to $3,160,351. As early as February 1981, efforts had already been made in the office of the vice president for administration and public affairs to save funds, including:

- Substantial staff reductions by combining the office of campus park and planning with the office of facilities planning and space manage- ment, and locating the new unit in one office.

- Substantial reduction in the grounds maintenance budget by eliminating all seasonal labor for the summer.

- Imposition of new parking rates to maintain all parking on campus on a self-supporting basis.

Services also were curtailed and some staff positions eliminated in offices overseen by the vice president for finance and operations and treasurer, producing a total savings of $2 million. In the controller's office, for example, travel advances were no longer issued for trips costing less than $750; ID cards no longer had photographs; the fee for spouse ID cards was raised from $3 to $7 and the revenue used to offset the cost of the student ID office; a central billing service was discon- tinued for departments with sufficient volume to warrant independent billing operations; and, finally, the registration period for winter and spring terms was reduced from five to three days, and outside personnel were no longer hired to help.

The university services division had to reduce its services further shortly after it successfully completed a program of staff reductions and improved services that had begun ten years earlier. Among new reduc- tions were a delay of up to a day in the processing of outgoing U.S. mail and elimination of a variety of special services, extensive delays in pro- cessing purchase orders, and discontinuance or modification of various general stores services.

Student Services

The division of student affairs and services tried to maintain its level of student services, but consequently had to make larger cuts in other areas and to reorganize its services. For example, funds for the student activities office were cut by more than $55,000, as compared to $28,704 for the student financial aid office, and residence hall counselors are now paid with auxiliary rather than general funds.

Academic Programs

Academic program reductions totaled $13,768,191. Over $2 million of these cuts were in administration. As an example, the provost's office reduced its budget by $1.6 million, eliminating an administrative faculty staff position, reducing and reorganizing its office of institutional research, placing the instructional media center on a self-supporting basis, and instituting other reductions. The office of the assistant provost for academic administration saved $554,000 through reorganization and budget reductions.

Within academic programs themselves, some core colleges incurred major reductions. The College of Arts and Letters reduced its budget by $970,022. Among other reductions, the department of humanities lost 7.50 faculty; the departments of linguistics and of German, Russian, Oriental, and African languages were merged; and the studio art program was curtailed.

The College of Natural Science instituted savings amounting to $1.2 million. Major savings occurred with elimination of the science and mathematics teaching center ($194,000), reduction or elimination of laboratories in the department of natural science ($350,500), and savings from retirements and open positions in selected departments ($202,600).

The College of Social Science also incurred reductions nearing $1 million, including elimination of all instructional programs in the Justin Morrill Inter-College program's instructional core. This elimination alone saved $348,124. The department of social science/general education also incurred a substantial reduction of $110,000.

The College of Education was another division that experienced heavy reductions, more than $1 million. Its largest reduction was in personnel, through retirements and open positions, for a total of $214,000. Its second largest cut was through administrative reorganization of the dean's office and the departments, for a savings of $212,000.

Even the Colleges of Medicine had substantial cuts. The College of Human Medicine reduced its budget by $1.4 million. It eliminated its funding for the School of Medical Technology, for a savings of $144,288, and substantially curtailed funding for its behavioral social science program ($116,390) and its Office of Medical Education Research and Development ($119,314). The college also designated program support funds to support ongoing commitments with its medical service plan and transferred $300,000 in faculty support from the general fund to the medical service plan to avoid additional faculty lay-offs.

The College of Osteopathic Medicine cut its funds by just over $1 million. Its major reductions were achieved by: eliminating the office of medical education, research, and development ($156,852), curtailing advising and other nonessential teaching efforts and support ($244,848), curtailing administration ($109,198), and reducing research support and the visiting professor program ($130,030).

Some colleges had less substantial cuts. The College of Business reduced its budget by $523,317, through such steps as elimination of the bureau of business and economic research ($188,791) and retirement of three full professors who were replaced by assistant professors, for a total savings of $26,010. Another $156,044 was saved by eliminating courses in the business education and office administration department. The College of Communication Arts and Sciences saved $134,000, largely by transferring significant numbers of faculty from an annual-year basis to an academic-year basis ($56,176), and by curtailing and eliminating other programs. In the College of Engineering, the budget was cut by $249,000. Reductions included savings of $75,000 in the college summer program, $25,000 in the lifelong education and cooperative education programs, and $40,000 in short-term research support in the division of engineering research.

Faculty and Staff Reductions

By declaring a "state of financial crisis" in February, MSU's board of trustees gave the university legal sanction to consider laying off tenured faculty who held their appointments until retirement, absent conditions of financial exigency. It was clear that MSU's financial crisis required savings in personnel costs, the largest expenditure for any institution of higher education.

Reductions-in-force called forth creative solutions to the painful process of deciding whom to lay off. Approximately 900 positions were eliminated, of which 250 were tenure system faculty and specialists with job security. Of these positions, about half were identified as vacancies, transfers, retirements, or resignations. Of remaining faculty positions, 111 were tenured faculty and 3 were tenure system faculty on probationary appointment. Table II shows how staff employment status changed.

Special retirement options and intra-university transfers were offered to affected employees. As a result, the massive task of reassignment and retrenchment was accomplished with these results:

- No tenured faculty member was terminated involuntarily.

- No specialist with job security was terminated involuntarily.

Table II

Total Personnel Options/Actions

	Total No.	Total %	Faculty No.	Faculty %	Specialists No.	Specialists %
1. Retirement—regular/ special	7	5.6	7	6.0	0	0
2. Voluntary resignation	3	2.4	3	2.6	0	0
3. Incentive plans/special retirement either immediately or after 1981–82	11	8.9	10	8.8	1	10.0
4. Incentive plans either immediately or after 1981–82	56	45.0	50	44.0	6	60.0
5. Part-time tenure (in curtailed units only)	6	4.9	6	5.3	0	0
6. Transfers to other units	13	10.5	13	11.4	0	0
7. Reassignments into open positions in other units	23	18.5	23	20.0	0	0
8. Nonrenewal of appointments of probationary faculty/ specialists	5	4.0	2	1.8	3	30.0
TOTAL	124	99.8*	114	99.9*	10	100.0

*Figures may not add up to 100% due to rounding.

- All tenure system faculty and specialists in the job security system on probationary appointments had terms of their appointments honored in full.

- Four tenured faculty from the original total remained as individuals with "no options selected." After consultation with these individuals and relevant academic units, they were reassigned to other university units that had continuing fund support.

- Between 230 and 240 tenure system and job security system positions have been or will be eliminated.

Two major considerations guided this personnel reduction process: assistance to tenured faculty and sustaining affirmative action commitments.

The university offered a variety of incentive retirement options to tenured faculty on a one-time basis only, to be chosen by August 31, 1981. To further ease problems, special retirement options were reinstated in February 1982 and were available until June 15, 1982. They included:

Unpaid Leave of Absence. An employee took a leave of absence without pay for up to two years, ending with retirement. Eligible employees had to be vested for retirement by the end of the period. They received the university's regular contribution toward health and dental insurance, but had to pay the cost of other optional benefits. They could begin to draw their retirement funds during this period.

Phased Retirement. Employees reduced their employment status to part-time. They also had to be vested for their retirement by the end of the period, not to exceed two years. The employee had to be employed for 50% of the time and for at least nine months during this phased period.

Early Retirement Salary Adjustment. Employees could be granted special salary increases which they could invest in TIAA-CREF to limit reduction in contract contributions resulting from early retirement. Eligibility requirements applied under this option were similar to those under other options.

Waiver of Retirement Options. In exceptional situations that would result in demonstrable savings, MSU would consider waiving minimum retirement requirements.

Throughout the budget reduction process, administrators and constituent groups agreed on the need to monitor the impact of reduction plans on employment progress for women and minorities. According to one administrator, "The goal was to move through the budget reduction process without any loss in the relative representation of women and minorities." It appears that the goal was achieved. There was an increase from 7.1% in fall 1980 to 7.6% in fall 1981 for minorities in the tenure system. Women increased from 13.4% to 13.6%. Minorities and nonminority women with continuing appointments (tenure system and job security) increased from 7% to 7.6% and from 18.3% to 19.1%, respectively. The percentage of minorities in the total academic person- nel system increased from 8.1 to 8.9. However, nonminority women in the total academic personnel system decreased from 23.7% to 23.2% because of a decrease in temporary faculty and staff. The hiring rate decreased, but the rate of reappointment was comparable to other years.

MSU achieved considerable success in persuading faculty that its plan for dealing with tenured personnel was compassionate and economically appropriate. One measure of its success is the favorable report on MSU policies in the March-April 1982 *Academe,* published by the American Association of University Professors ("Preserving Tenure: Com- mitments in Hard Times, The Michigan State Experience," by Mordechai Kreinin).

Summary

Michigan State University was the first major institution to deal with retrenchment during the late 1970s and early 1980s. It had neither guidelines nor theoretical models to follow in shaping a retrenchment process. However, its experiences are instructive in suggesting some policies and practices to help other institutions. In particular:

- *MSU established and sustained the idea that the key issue was centrality of programs to the institution's role and mission.*

- *Long-run costs and benefits were evaluated before reductions occurred.* For example, libraries did not receive as large a reduc- tion as other areas for fear that such cuts would impair the institution over the long haul.

- *Some units received more funds to help MSU get through this difficult period.* Development activities were increased, starting with a number of small capital campaigns. This commitment of funds during cutbacks enabled the university to raise $9 million.

- *Communication among all staff of the university improved.* The administration frankly stated MSU's problems and invited campuswide participation. Academic and business areas of MSU developed a team approach.

- *The governance process was strengthened.* Faculty and staff worked together under tight deadlines to produce a reduction plan.

The experience of Michigan State University demonstrates that, while retrenchment can be traumatic, it can also lead to thorough assessment of an institution's long-term role and mission. Such assessment can result in a reallocation process that can strengthen the quality of academic and support programs and enable an institution to respond effectively to future challenges.

References

Academic Programs: Michigan State University (university document, January 1983). Interprets mission statement and provides guidance on planning process.

Coordinated Proposals: Recommendations to the Board of Trustees (university document, March 22, 1981). Recommendations for program changes in academic areas.

Implementation of Modified Coordinated Proposal: Actions Affecting Individuals Appointed in the Academic Personnel System (university document, January 6, 1982).

Planning—Draft Materials (university document, January 1981). (Initial document describing budget reduction procedures—later modified, but basic thrust adhered to.)

"Preserving Tenure: Commitments in Hard Times, The Michigan State Experience," by Mordechai Kreinin. *Academe,* March-April 1982.

Statement on Long-Range Planning at Michigan State University (university document, January 1983).

The University of Michigan-Ann Arbor

In simplest terms...no more than the conventional and prudent practice of maintaining sufficient financial liquidity so that if revenues fall, or expenditures increase unexpectedly, monies can be found to fill the gap. That gives the organization time to adjust, it avoids crisis management and sudden disruptions in operations which might cause permanent and irreparable damage...

As an institution, we are choosing to give up something (a modest fraction of our size and scope) in order to meet other higher priorities...

The opening observations from Harold T. Shapiro, president, and Billy E. Frye, vice-president for academic affairs, describe the rationale that has guided the University of Michigan through reallocation and retrenchment since the late 1970s.

Since the early seventies, it has been clear that the university would not continue to receive the level of state support it had previously enjoyed. In 1970–71, Michigan's governor withheld budgeted funds from state agencies in order to balance the budget, and the university had to levy a 1% midyear budget reduction on all its units and request them to prepare for a 3% cut in the following year's base budget.

In 1977, Harold Shapiro, now president of the University of Michigan, became vice-president for academic affairs on the Ann Arbor campus. That position carried with it the chairmanship of the committee on budget administration, making him chief budget officer for the university's general fund. Under his direction, planning, budgeting, and evaluation activities that had occurred separately in earlier years became one integrated process and a clear purpose for planning emerged: the reallocation of scarce resources.

This case study describes how the University of Michigan-Ann Arbor made such reallocation decisions.

Institutional Profile

The University of Michigan is a major institution with significant commitments in undergraduate and graduate education, professional education, advanced research training, and scholarships. The Ann Arbor campus enrolls about 35,000 students, almost all of whom are full-time; about two-thirds are undergraduates. Enrollment today is about 1,600 students fewer than in 1972–73. Instructional staff numbers about 4,500, with 2,200 serving as full-time faculty. The remainder are graduate teaching fellows and adjunct staff. The university is known for having one of the most distinguished faculties in the country, a reputation enabled in part by extremely generous state appropriations beginning in the 1870s.

Early reductions did not seriously affect the university's efforts to carry out programs in its areas of commitment. The revenue situation for academic programs, however, gradually deteriorated from 1972–73 to 1982–83. In 1972–73, 43.3% or $130.6 million of total university revenues of $301.4 million were from the Ann Arbor general fund. In 1982–83, the university had income of $759.4 million, of which $277.8 million, or 36.6%, came from the Ann Arbor general fund. In 1983, this fund paid for 57.2% of core instructional and research budgets, although this state support accounted for only 30.5% of the total educational and general budget. State support for educational and general declined from 37.8% in 1972–73 to 30.5% in 1982–83. These figures do not include medical activities (hospital and professional fees) in the auxiliary activities fund, which increased from $62 million in 1972–73 to $263.6 million in 1982–83.

In 1982–83, the university general fund received $132 million in state appropriations, $120 million in student fees, $23 million from the federal government, and $3 million in other funds. For the decade 1973–1983, student fees' contribution rose from 29% of total revenues to 43%; state appropriations declined from 61% to 47.5%.

In the university's more recent history, reallocation has occurred in two distinct periods. The first period started in 1977 when the "priority fund" was established for three years to give the university budgetary flexibility so that it could effectively respond to emerging financial problems. Under this fund, units returned approximately 1% of their budget to central administration; these funds were, in turn, reallocated back into base budgets. Over the life of the funds, money was generally reallocated from noninstructional units and noninstructional functions within academic units into instructional functions. Within schools and colleges, reductions in the first year tended to occur in central collegiate accounts. However, in successive years, reductions occurred increasingly in subsidiary units of colleges.

Requests from various units for priority fund allocations were similar to normal budget requests, most being for a single year. Also, there were more requests for faculty and staff than for nonsalary items, and more for improving existing programs than for developing new ones.

Following a budget crisis spawned by declines in the state economy in 1980–81, during which severe reductions occurred, the university began its second reallocation effort. In 1982, it established the "five-year plan," a concept similar to the priority fund in that it also captures funds from units for reallocation by the central administration. This time, however, more severe reductions of some units have been anticipated due to perceived future problems such as declining enrollment, accumulated delayed maintenance and equipment costs, and modest state appropriations.

In both internal and external activities, the university now focuses on using resources effectively through reallocation. Within this overall framework, however, it has had to deal with budgetary crises similar to those faced by institutions in other beleaguered states.

Chronology

The history of the University of Michigan's reallocation experiences differs somewhat from that of many other institutions that have undergone budget reductions. At those institutions, budgetary decisions dominate the story in the sense that retrenchment consisted basically of cost-cutting measures in response to cutbacks in state appropriations. At the University of Michigan, the reallocation process *itself* is as important as specific reduction measures. Establishment of the priority fund in 1977, before any severe reductions in state appropriations actually occurred, reflects the anticipatory nature of the university's approach to retrenchment.

There are four significant developments in Michigan's experience with reallocation:

First. In 1977, the university introduced the priority fund, the first universitywide mechanism for reallocation. The fund was established for a three-year period primarily to achieve budgetary flexibility.

Second. In fall 1980, the university faced a major budgetary shortfall, following a series of disappointments regarding state appropriations. Earlier in January, the governor had announced a proposed 9.5% increase for higher education, and university administrators projected an appropriation of about $138 million, which would not have kept up with the rate of inflation but was still $12 million more than the previous appropriation. This proposed 9.5% increase was scaled down to a projected 3% increase, on the basis of which the university drew up a budget incorporating a 9% increase in faculty salaries. Appropriations for 1980–81 were not approved until after the fall elections, nearly six months after the beginning of the university's fiscal year. It later became apparent that the appropriation was likely to be 96% of the previous year's sum, or 4% lower than the university's worst expectations. The final state appropriation in December 1980 was one percentage point lower than the anticipated 4% reduction, producing an extra $3 million shortfall on top of the $9 million deficit expected earlier (based on the assumed 3% state appropriation increase). To accommodate these shortfalls, the university reduced 1980–81 expenditures and enacted some base budget reductions going into the 1981–82 fiscal year.

Third. In February 1982, the university introduced a new five-year reallocation plan to produce $20 million, or about 7.5% of the 1981–82 general fund budget, that would revert to the central administration for reallocation to high priority concerns.

Fourth. By August 1982, the university had to brace itself for still another series of state-ordered reductions due to a $150 million deficit in state budget. The university anticipated this shortfall and prepared for the contingency by freezing major expenditures in selected central accounts.

Table I provides an overview of reallocation at the University of Michigan.

Table I

Chronology

Date	Action
1977	The "priority fund" is established to reallocate resources through a "tax" on units within the university. Fund resources over three years expected to total $3.8 million.
January 1980	Governor announces a proposed 9.5% increase in state appropriations for higher education.
Summer 1980	With state revenues declining, the university prepares budget based on an assumed 3% increase in appropriations over the previous year and a 9% increase in faculty salaries.
September 1980	University learns that it will probably get 96% of the previous year's appropriation, yielding a $9 million budget shortfall. Legislature still does not set appropriation. Each unit prepares contingency plans.
October 1980	Administration deals with immediate shortfall by cutting $6 million from equipment purchases and other central accounts until next fiscal year and preparing all units to cut salary budgets by 6% for the next fiscal year.
December 1980	Actual appropriation reduction is 5%, creating an additional $3 million shortfall. Selective cuts made in institutional support units.
February 1982	The "five-year plan" to produce $20 million over five years announced. Central administration to reallocate these funds.
Summer 1982	$5 million captured for reallocation into faculty salaries; three major reviews of schools and colleges initiated.
Summer 1983	A total of $4 million, captured from reductions in all units, reallocated into several areas, including special market adjustments for faculty and staff, instructional equipment, and graduate financial aid.

Approaches to Reallocation and Retrenchment

The University of Michigan has stressed the importance of reallocation rather than retrenchment only in its efforts to adapt to its changing
financial situation. Therefore, when units of the university are asked to
examine their activities and to decide on priorities, they are to determine
what should be improved or sustained as well as what would be cut
back. To the fullest extent possible, the university has sought to have
funds available to achieve its goals.

First Reallocation Effort: The Priority Fund

When the priority fund was established in December 1977, the
university declared:

> It is vital that the university maintain its ability, even through periods of
> stable real-dollar budgets, to adapt to (the) changing interests (of students
> and faculty, the development of new areas of knowledge, and the interests
> of society), as well as to assist existing programs which are, in view of our
> priorities, relatively underfunded. *Budgetary flexibility is an essential ingre-*
> *dient of the ability to respond to both of these challenges.* (emphasis added)

Various changes during the 1970s pointed to the need for budgetary
flexibility. The period of sustained growth in the 1960s was succeeded
by a period of declining state support, owing to general economic difficulties, and of institutional cost increases. Despite a variety of
measures undertaken to deal with these conditions, such as ad hoc
across-the-board reductions, significant tuition increases, and deferral of
maintenance expenditures, it became clear by 1977 that there was inadequate slack in the budget. There was a need for alternative strategies
to maintain or improve program quality over the coming decade within a
stable, real-dollar budget, and the differential multi-year reallocation procedure known as the "priority fund" arose from this need. The fund was
one means of helping units implement a large evaluation and planning
effort that had been initiated several years earlier.

Under terms of the fund, which was established for three years
subject to re-evaluation, each unit's base general fund budget was
reduced by 1% of the previous year's budget. In effect, this was an
annual tax on base budgets. The university anticipated savings of
approximately $1 million, $1.3 million, and $1.5 million in the three-year
period. This money would then be reallocated into base budgets of
selected units, depending on university priorities.

There were two exceptions to this general plan. First, staff benefits,
purchased utilities, and mandatory transfers were not included in reductions. Second, research and instruction budgets of academic units were

reduced at a more gradual pace over a three-year period. Starting with 1978–79, these budgets were reduced each year by .333%, .666%, and 1%, respectively.

At the outset of the process, the university cited criteria to be used for reallocation decisions. Among these were:

- Program's centrality to university, viewed in terms of its pertinence to and support of growth, preservation, and communication of knowledge.

- Current and projected future societal demands for graduates and/or services of program.

- Impact on university's relationship with community, other universities, and governments.

- Current reputation and quality of program, considering national ratings, professional accreditation standards, research productivity, qualification of entering students, quality of graduate placement, and attrition of students.

Initially, priority fund procedures required that units submit their requests for reallocation from the priority fund to the vice president for academic affairs (also chairman of the committee on budget administration), at least two weeks before the unit's annual budget conference, scheduled during February and March; reallocation decisions were announced in May. This schedule made it difficult for units to recruit faculty and to plan programs for the coming year. To alleviate this problem, the unified request and planning/budgeting conferences were moved to early fall, before the primary recruiting season, and, whenever possible, a partial allocation of priority funds was made in the fall to assist in recruiting.

The committee on budget administration was advised by the budget priorities committee, a group that included nine faculty members chosen by the faculty senate, two vice presidents chosen by the president, two deans appointed by the vice president for academic affairs, and two students chosen by the student assembly.

Unit heads responded to necessary reductions in different ways. Some made across-the-board cuts in programs and departments. Others made differential cuts, usually focusing on nonsalary accounts that were already underfunded when compared to salaries. In the first year, large schools and colleges tended to absorb much of the reduction in their collegiate accounts. In the second and third years, these schools and colleges took reductions that were both larger and more selective from their subsidiary units.

The priority fund concept fostered reallocations in the first two years, as the fund was phased in; noninstructional budgets were taxed more heavily than instructional budgets. Also, schools and colleges received much more from the fund than did support units.

A need recognized by the central administration and by some units was to move dollars from salary to nonsalary uses. To accomplish this and provide incentives, the central administration gave multi-year grants to selected units for equipment. It was understood that units would match priority fund allocations with further internal reallocation, thereby building up equipment accounts more rapidly.

The priority fund produced many beneficial effects. It facilitated academic program planning both from the central and the college perspective. Knowing that reductions were needed for at least three successive years caused units to engage in more long-term academic and fiscal planning and to retain some budget flexibility. Schools and colleges gained more leverage with programs and departments, mostly in terms of reallocation of faculty positions. By providing a margin of new dollars, fund allocations helped in the implementation of program plans for some units. On the other hand, some nonacademic units raised, or attempted to raise, their fees to compensate for priority fund reductions, which defeated in part the fund's purposes. Fee raises of this nature tended to occur in areas where it was possible to impose increases in application or service fees and internal recharge rates, such as computer services and physical plant maintenance. Other units indicated some charges for services that had previously been provided at no cost to recipient units.

Reallocation Becomes Retrenchment

In 1980, this qualitative approach to constrained financial resources faced a major obstacle: Michigan's deteriorating economic situation made it difficult for the state government to decide on appropriations for higher education until well into the institution's fiscal year. Among other factors, plummeting auto sales had multiple effects in terms of declining state revenues on the one hand and increasing expenditures for unemployment payments on the other.

By June 1980, the university realized that its state appropriation might increase by as little as 3%. Counting on this amount, it decided to go ahead with a budget that incorporated a 9% faculty salary increase. The university was particularly concerned about losing faculty to other comparable research institutions if the raise did not go through. It also knew, however, that any smaller state appropriation would require all units to reduce their budgets. In fact, this commitment to increasing faculty salaries seriously impaired the university's flexibility in responding to further cuts.

In anticipation of further reductions, the university asked all units to develop contingency plans detailing how they could cut their budgets by 1, 2, or 0% depending on the final state appropriation. These plans were too optimistic: the state appropriation was projected as being closer to 96% of the previous year's figure, and the university had to cut $9 million from its budget immediately in the fall. Three million dollars of this reduction came from units' contingency plans based on 0% increase. Another six million dollars came from deferring equipment purchases and other centrally controlled expenses.

Having faced a number of unanticipated budget reductions, the administration decided that it had to develop plans for base reductions for the 1981–82 fiscal year. At the same time, it decided to include a provision for reallocation of funds in reduction plans. In October 1980, all university units were asked to submit plans for a 6% reduction that would yield approximately $9.2 million, one million more than the anticipated shortfall. Additional funds would be distributed among particularly needy units. Schools and colleges had just four weeks to comply; furthermore, they were not permitted to hire any employees until their particular reduction plan was approved.

Units used several approaches to arrive at mandatory 6% reductions. In some cases, for example, faculty salaries were moved from general funds. Some faculty appointments were changed from an annual to an academic-year basis, and vacant positions were not filled. Some adjunct and part-time staff were notified that they would not be reappointed for the following year.

Some units found relief from drastic reductions, however, when their pleas were heeded by the administration. The College of Literature, Science, and Arts' $2.2 million budget cut was eased by $300,000, and it later received a one-time-only grant of $340,000. The Law School's reduction of $202,000 was trimmed to just under $40,000. Pharmacy's reduction of $73,000 was dropped to $36,000, and Engineering had its scheduled reduction of $629,000 completely eliminated.

Efforts to cover anticipated budget reductions, however, proved to be insufficient. When the university finally received its state appropriation in December 1980, it was still another 1% below the previously expected 4% reduction, an additional $3 million shortfall. This time, the university made selective and deep cuts in a few nonacademic units. The Center for Research on Learning and Teaching was reduced by $100,000; the Michigan media program lost $200,000; recreational sports lost $130,000; and radio station WUOM lost $100,000. The largest cut came in the extension service, down by $1.2 million from a total budget of $1.9 million. This reduction virtually gutted the separately budgeted extension service program; greater responsibility was transferred to individual schools and colleges.

There is general agreement within the university that many cuts made during the 1980–81 budget crisis were not as effective as they would have been had they been made under less time pressure. On the whole, however, administrators felt that the crisis was handled well. Further-more, the 1980–81 budget cuts were viewed as only the beginning of a long process of internal reallocation of funds from lower to higher prior-ity programs.

A New Reallocation Plan

Following these retrenchment decisions for 1981–82, long-term plan-ning for reallocation began once again. Such planning is considered essential because the future outlook indicates that the current most critical problem—declining state support—is likely to continue due to a projected demographic decline of 20 to 30% in the traditional college-age population. Furthermore, from the university's viewpoint, these prob-lems are likely to be further compounded by reduced flexibility for internal reallocation because of several factors: (1) low staff turnover rate, (2) increasing proportion of tenured faculty, (3) continued accumulation of delayed maintenance and equipment costs that will become increasingly urgent, (4) continued problems with inflation, and (5) continued uncertainty regarding federal funding.

In February 1982, the vice president for academic affairs issued new instructions for a five-year reallocation plan to free $20 million, or about 7.5% of the 1981–82 general fund budget, for new or increased funding of targeted activities. There will be no net reduction in the university's general fund budget base as a result of this program. The goal is to reallocate, on average, at least $4 million per year, which is approxi-mately 2% of the academic and administrative and support units' budget; reductions are to occur at the earliest reasonable time in the five-year cycle.

The vice president identified six programmatic (rather than organiza-tional) areas as beneficiaries of reallocation: (1) salaries for faculty and staff, (2) research, including generation of better incentives for research, (3) undergraduate teaching and incentives for better teaching, (4) im-proved level of merit-based support for graduate students, (5) funds to regenerate budgetary capacity to respond to new intellectual developments and social needs, and to provide for selected program growth and development, and (6) improved level of support for instructional and research equipment and renovation of physical plant.

With funds returned to the central administration under this plan, the university could transfer money to priority areas, using normal budgetary decision-making and governance procedures. Units would be required to submit requests for support in high-priority areas; the vice president for academic affairs, with assistance from the budget priorities committee and committee on budget administration, would then redistribute funds to budgetary units. Funds would not be reallocated across-the-board, but would be distributed differentially based on quality, merit, need, and new intellectual development.

The new reallocation process is based on two categories of reductions: large reductions in selective program areas or closures, and variable-shared reductions (VSR) in all other units. The first approach applies to reductions that exceed 20 to 30% of a unit's budget over the five-year period. Variable-shared reductions will occur in all units that are not in the first category. For instructional functions of most schools and colleges, VSRs will range from 0–10%, averaging 5% over the period. For administrative and support units, the VSRs will range from 5 to 15%, averaging over 10% during the period. The reallocation plan therefore continues the trend of shifting resources from administrative and support functions to instruction and research.

Under the new reallocation process, major budget reductions in selected academic programs began in early 1983. Some specific program reductions were: Extension—$123,000 (one-half of the remaining program); Institute of Labor and Industrial Relations—$106,000; and the Institute for Study of Mental Retardation—$290,000 (elimination of the entire program).

The process followed the basic procedure outlined in the "Regental Program Discontinuance Guidelines," which were used in program reviews in 1980–81. The vice president for academic affairs, with assistance from the budget priorities committee and committee on budget administration, developed a list of programs for which it was reasonable to propose major budget reductions or closure in light of criteria stated in the regental guidelines. Each identified unit was reviewed by a faculty-student committee functioning as a subcommittee of the budget priorities committee; all review committee members were from outside the unit being reviewed. The budget priorities committee assessed the subcommittee report and submitted its evaluation and recommendations, including possible alternatives, to the vice president for academic affairs who, with the committee on budget administration, made either a final decision or a recommendation to the board, as appropriate.

Procedures were provided for participation by the unit being reviewed and for obtaining views of others in the university community—and other interested or affected parties—through letters and both public and private hearings. There were already students on the budget priorities committee; further student participation in specific reviews was encouraged where appropriate.

There may be circumstances, particularly in institutional support areas, when these procedures are not the most appropriate for making necessary budget adjustments. In such instances, the appropriate vice president may devise more suitable alternative procedures in consulta' tion with the corresponding faculty advisory committee, budget priorities committee, and committee on budget administration.

Initially, three schools—Art, Natural Resources, and Educa' tion—were targeted for major selective program reduction. After review and once a reduction target is set—40% reduction in the School of Education, for example—a faculty transition team in the affected school is given two to three months to develop a plan for phasing in the reduc' tion over three to five years. The faculty plan then is submitted to the central administration for review, and negotiations follow to develop a final plan.

Thus far, the university has reallocated $9 million dollars under the five'year plan. In 1982–83, $5 million in reductions from instructional and noninstructional units were reallocated to faculty salaries. Faculty salary increases, it should be noted, are based on merit and are not across'the'board. In the 1983–84 budget, $4 million captured from reductions in all units were targeted for distribution into several areas: merit support for graduate students ($1 million), instructional equipment ($1 million), library acquisitions ($500,000), academic program develop' ment ($500,000), and special market adjustments for faculty and staff ($1 million).

Summary

When this case study was completed in spring 1983, the University of Michigan at Ann Arbor still had major steps remaining to complete the last three years of the reallocation plan. Therefore, this case study is useful principally for describing how a large university approached the process of planning for reallocation, rather than for what it has already accomplished.

Senior administrators who were interviewed stressed that reallocation and retrenchment depend first and foremost on an institution's review and assessment of its purpose as well as its current and future situation. This process at the University of Michigan focused on three questions:

1. How does the university perceive its role and mission?

2. What are the university's resources in terms of funds, faculty, and programs?

3. How long does the university believe the state's economic problems will continue?

The University of Michigan's responses to these questions are clearly reflected in the way it approached reallocation first in 1977 and again in 1982. First, the university sees itself as a major research institution that serves both state and national interests through the high quality of its faculty and programs. High quality is considered the key to sustaining institutional role and mission. Second, the university assessed itself to determine which areas and programs should be reduced and which should receive recaptured money. Third, the university viewed the state's economic problems as long-term in nature, and consequently it developed first a three-year and then a five-year reallocation plan to deal with budgetary consequences of these problems. Programs are to be reduced over a three- to five-year period and funds saved thereby are to be reallocated to insure that the University of Michigan can sustain its position as a major educational resource.

Internal reallocation of resources at the University of Michigan comprised the first of three action plans devised to deal with what is foreseen to be a continuing rather than a temporary problem—scarce resources, primarily in terms of dwindling state support. The other two plans consist of renewed efforts to strengthen the partnership between state and university and a greatly enhanced program of private support through gifts and endowments. Further, the university has engaged in significant efforts to reduce expenses, particularly in energy areas, and has taken steps to insure that nongeneral fund activities pay for services provided by general fund units.

The significance of the reallocation plan is that it is a self-help measure with an overall positive thrust: it represents a continued commitment to preserve the university's long tradition of excellence through deployment of existing resources to areas of greatest merit and promise, rather than through the more short-term measure of "shared austerity" which the administration felt would be detrimental to the quality of the institution as a whole. Furthermore, the University of Michigan's approach to declining financial resources is anticipatory rather than reactive in nature and, in effect, enables the university to make informed, though still difficult, choices.

References

"Discontinuance of Academic Programs" (guidelines) Minutes of Board of Regents meeting; October 1979.

"How the Cuts Were Made" by Don Hunt, *Ann Arbor Observer,* September 1981.

"Operating with Resource Constraints—Some Reflections." Paper presented at the Association of American Universities meeting, October 18, 1982, in St. Louis, Missouri, by Harold T. Shapiro, President, University of Michigan.

"Resource Allocation: Stopgap or Support for Academic Planning?" by R. Sue Mims, *New Directions for Institutional Research.* No. 28, 1980.